Finally, a clear and accurate treatise of a subject few ministers tackle today. *Breaking Curses, Experiencing Healing* is your key to freedom, with explanations for what really goes on in the spiritual realm.

—*Keith and Mary Hudson*
Keith Hudson Ministries

Pastor Tom Brown has hit the mark with *Breaking Curses, Experiencing Healing*. He deals with the complete spectrum of physical, mental, and emotional diseases, as well as the destructive issue of homosexuality. In doing so, I believe Tom addresses the real reasons why a person deals with cross-gender feelings, as well as the steps to overcome this identity crisis. This is a must-read for anyone struggling with diseases that may have a spiritual root.

Jim Willoughby
al Convention of
Faith Ministries

The vast majority of Christians today are almost completely ignorant of the nature of evil spirits. Because many pastors are fearful of things they do not understand, they choose to ignore this portion of Christ's ministry. As a result, multitudes of people—including Christians—are needlessly living in torment.

Many contemporary pastors have rejected the idea that Christians can have a demon, thereby eliminating the section of Jesus' Great Commission that instructs believers to *"heal the sick"* and *"cast out demons"* (Matthew 10:8 NKJV).

I believe that Pastor Tom Brown has answered a call to minister to the sick, afflicted, and tormented with an emphasis on the casting out of demons that is comparable to that of the New Testament church.

—*Dr. Bill Basansky*
Former Trustee, International Convention of
Faith Ministries

BREAKING CURSES

Experiencing
Healing

BREAKING CURSES

Experiencing

Healing

Tom BROWN

WHITAKER
HOUSE

Unless otherwise indicated, Scripture quotations are from the *Holy Bible, New International Version*®, NIV®, © 1973, 1978, 1984 by the International Bible Society. Used by permission of Zondervan. All rights reserved. Scripture quotations marked (AMP) are taken from the *Amplified*® *Bible*, © 1954, 1958, 1962, 1964, 1965, 1987 by The Lockman Foundation. Used by permission. (www.Lockman.org) Scripture quotations marked (ASV) are from the American Standard Edition of the Revised Version of the Holy Bible. Scripture quotations marked (TLB) are taken from *The Living Bible*, © 1971. Used by permission of Tyndale House Publishers, Inc., Wheaton, Illinois 60189. All rights reserved.

Some Hebrew and Greek words are taken from *Strong's Exhaustive Concordance*. Unless otherwise indicated, all word definitions are taken from *Merriam-Webster's 11th Collegiate Dictionary*.

BREAKING CURSES, EXPERIENCING HEALING

Tom Brown
P.O. Box 27275
El Paso, TX 79926
(915) 855-9673 / www.tbm.org

ISBN: 978-1-60374-263-4
Printed in the United States of America
© 2011 by Tom Brown

Whitaker House
1030 Hunt Valley Circle
New Kensington, PA 15068
www.whitakerhouse.com

Library of Congress Cataloging-in-Publication Data

Brown, Tom, 1963–

Breaking curses, experiencing healing / Tom Brown.

   p. cm.

   ISBN 978-1-60374-263-4 (trade pbk. : alk. paper) 1. Spiritual healing. 2. Healing—Religious aspects—Christianity. 3. Spiritual warfare. I. Title.

BT732.5.B77 2011

234'.131—dc22

                         2010046391

3 4 5 6 7 8 9 10 11 12 ᴜᴜ 19 18 17 16 15 14 13 12

Acknowledgments

There are always many people to thank when a book is published. First, I am grateful to my church members for allowing me to share the revelation of this book. I knew the message was life changing by your receptivity. Then, there are my proofreaders: Shirleen Ledoux, Sue Mitchell, and Fernie Rodriguez. I appreciate your invaluable suggestions.

Thanks to my children, Justin, Faith, and Caleb, who think I spend too much time on the computer. You see, I really am doing work!

And how could I ever forget the wife of my youth? Thank you, Sonia, for always encouraging me and providing your personal insights in order to make a book better.

Of course, without the Lord, how could I ever accomplish anything? Thank You, Lord, for counting me faithful in service for You. The worst day in the ministry is better than the best day in the world.

Contents

Part III: Spiritual Diseases

Part IV: The Evidence

Introduction

Millions saw it. Some were dumbfounded, others skeptical. Still more were impressed.

The television camera zoomed in on Lori's face as the demon screamed through her voice, "No! No! No!" She was writhing on her back, her hands swinging back and forth, punching and grabbing as if she were a puppet and someone else was pulling the strings.

By all accounts, Lori appeared to be a normal thirty-two-year-old woman. She had a regular job and many friends, but, like many others, she faced unbearable depression.

"I'm constantly depressed," she told the MSNBC reporters. She had been on medication for depression but was certain that her condition was being caused by demonic activity. She had asked me—her pastor—to pray deliverance over her.

I did not want this to become a circus. Deliverance is a personal thing, yet, at the same time, the Bible tells us that Jesus often delivered people from demons in public settings. So, you can understand my reluctance—as well as my cautious willingness—to allow an MSNBC television crew to film the actual deliverance. I did not want anyone to be embarrassed. I agreed to allow them in the service provided anyone they filmed gave written permission for their footage to be used in the final program.

Lori had agreed not only to be filmed but also to be interviewed prior to the deliverance. She told the reporters of the many years she had suffered from excruciating depression. She testified that strange, unexplainable marks had been found on her body. The reporters also noted the medication she had been taking. For the network, Lori was the ideal subject for a documentary on exorcism: someone who not only claimed to be possessed by demons, but who was also available to be interviewed before and after the deliverance.

As the cameras rolled on that Sunday morning, Lori came forward for prayer. She stood on the platform, and all I could think to do was point my finger at her and say, "I command you, spirits, to name yourselves, in the name of Jesus Christ of Nazareth—the Son of God." Lori bowed her head, wrapped her arms around her body, and began to sob uncontrollably. Soon, she was prostrate on the floor and sobbing even louder.

I felt I knew which spirits were in her. "I command all thoughts of suicide, all thoughts of lust, anger, bitterness, and self-pity to come out! You will all come out. I called you by name!"

Soon, Lori was calm. A grin came across her olive-skinned face. She was free. In five minutes, the deliverance was over.

Afterward, she described to reporters what it had felt like: "It was the most unusual thing I have ever experienced." The important thing was the result. Two days later, the watchful, scrutinizing MSNBC reporters admitted that Lori was no longer experiencing the symptoms of depression.

"I don't have to take pills. I can handle everyday problems," Lori delighted to say. Since her freedom, Lori continues to serve the Lord with all her heart to this day.

Of course, as in all cases of deliverance, there is no guarantee of permanent results. Jesus Himself once warned that spirits might come back to make the person worse. (See Matthew 12:43–45.)

Toward the end of their documentary, MSNBC admitted that some people do seem to get better after spiritual deliverance. Although psychologists may attribute the success to psychological release, hypnotism, or positive faith on the part of the delivered, my hope is that more professionals will acknowledge the efforts of the men and women of God who are attempting to rid people of their demons through prayer and the Word of God.

What This Book Will Do for You

Since that MSNBC documentary aired, I have received many calls, letters, and e-mails from people around the world asking for deliverance.[1] Many simply have questions about exorcism and demons. Since then, I have been interviewed many times on national television, as well as on the British Broadcasting Company, on a wide range of questions about deliverance. It is because of all this interest that I have decided to write this book.

In it, I have attempted to answer questions about deliverance and to provide sound, logical, and scriptural teaching as to its scope and value. It is my hope and prayer that through this book, you will:

- Learn how to tell the difference between natural and demonic sicknesses.

- Discover what a generational curse is, how it can bring sickness into your life, and, most important, how to break it.

- Receive a revelation of your complete healing through the redemptive atonement of Jesus Christ.

- Acquire the knowledge of deliverance necessary concerning yourself, as well as the knowledge

---

[1] Author's note: The MSNBC documentary was originally aired in 2001; however, it has been re-aired multiple times over the years.

of what it means for you to be body, soul, and spirit, and how this relates to Satan's attacks.

• Spot the works of Satan and know how to stop him.

• Find out what the occult is and how to avoid being subtly enticed into the realm of the spirits of darkness.

• Recognize Satan's number one trap and how you can escape it.

• Be challenged to have your own ministry of deliverance.

• Be inspired with real stories of people who received healing through deliverance.

How This Book Is Arranged

I have divided this book into four sections. The first three sections cover the three compartments of health: physical, mental, and spiritual. I will show the need to be healed in all three areas and uncover ways in which demons can make people sick in each one.

The fourth section deals with common objections people raise concerning the ministry of deliverance. I will make an important defense for the need to have both a truth encounter and a power encounter if people are going to be delivered. I conclude this section with stories of real people from my church who received healing when they were delivered from evil spirits.

I encourage you to read your Bible along with this book, because what is important is not my opinion but what the Bible teaches about deliverance. You can look up the Scripture references yourself to verify whether or not they are saying what I maintain they are saying. I have nothing to hide. If what I write is not scriptural, challenge me. Of course, you will have to challenge me with Scripture, since my beliefs are derived solely from the Bible.

I hope you will find the answers and scriptural knowledge you are looking for. Ultimately, it is my desire that this book provide the healing you need—a healing that is often available only through deliverance.

Part I

Physical Diseases

Chapter One

Sickness and the Role of Demons

One Sabbath, while Jesus was teaching in one of the synagogues, a woman who had been crippled by a spirit for eighteen years approached.

On a Sabbath Jesus was teaching in one of the synagogues, and a woman was there who had been crippled by a spirit for eighteen years. She was bent over and could not straighten up at all. When Jesus saw her, he called her forward and said to her, "Woman, you are set free from your infirmity." Then he put his hands on her, and immediately she straightened up and praised God. Indignant because Jesus had healed on the Sabbath, the synagogue ruler said to the people, "There are six days for work. So come and be healed on those days, not on the Sabbath." The Lord answered

him, "You hypocrites! Doesn't each of you on the Sabbath untie his ox or donkey from the stall and lead it out to give it water? Then should not this woman, a daughter of Abraham, whom Satan has kept bound for eighteen long years, be set free on the Sabbath day from what bound her?"
(Luke 13:10–16)

On another occasion, a man knelt before Jesus, saying,

"Lord, have mercy on my son....He has seizures and is suffering greatly. He often falls into the fire or into the water. I brought him to your disciples, but they could not heal him." "O unbelieving and perverse generation," Jesus replied, "how long shall I stay with you? How long shall I put up with you? Bring the boy here to me." Jesus rebuked the demon, and it came out of the boy, and he was healed from that moment.
(Matthew 17:15–18)

> **While I am not saying that every disease is caused by demons, I do see a desperate need for both natural and demonic healing.**

There is definitely a relationship between healing and deliverance. In my travels around the world, I have discovered that many people never receive healing because they never received deliverance from the spirits that made

them sick in the first place. While I am not saying that every disease is caused by demons, I do
see a desperate need for both natural and demonic healing.

> *That evening after sunset the people brought
> to Jesus all the sick and demon-possessed.
> The whole town gathered at the door, and
> Jesus healed many who had various dis-
> eases. He also drove out many demons, but
> he would not let the demons speak because
> they knew who he was.* (Mark 1:32–34)

In this passage, note that Jesus accom-
plished two things: He healed many who were
sick with various diseases, and He cast out
many demons. Some people simply need natural healing from the diseases that have made
them sick; others, however, are in need of spiritual deliverance from the spirits that have made
them sick.

For many, the suggestion that demons could
be the cause of sickness may sound radical. If
you are among them, perhaps you are in need
of a radical approach to healing.

There are others who would caution me at
this point and say, "Pastor Tom, we need balance." I agree! I believe in balance; however,
to some, balance means compromising by ig-
noring deliverance completely. That is not how
Jesus achieved balance. Jesus achieved balance
by being extreme on all sides. He taught:

- extreme love

  If someone strikes you on the right cheek, turn to him the other also. (Matthew 5:39)

- extreme holiness

  If your right eye causes you to sin, gouge it out and throw it away. (Matthew 5:29)

- extreme faith

  If you have faith as small as a mustard seed, you can say to this mountain, "Move from here to there" and it will move.
  (Matthew 17:20)

- extreme evangelism

  Go into all the world and preach the good news to all creation. (Mark 16:15)

- and even extreme deliverance

  In my name they will drive out demons.
  (Mark 16:17)

Balance is not achieved by watering down the fundamentals of the Christian faith. When we do that, we achieve a lukewarm Christianity, and I think people are tired of tepid faith. The Bible provides a radical approach to healing as far as modern thinking is concerned—including the modern thinking of some born-again believers.

During the 1960s, when the deliverance movement was at its peak, many Christians had a tendency to see demons behind every bush.

Every problem anyone had was attributed to a demon, from the flu to overeating. Now, with the church's de-emphasis on the devil and demons, you no longer have to look behind bushes for demons—they can parade down the streets unnoticed. When was the last time you went to a Christian conference where there was a seminar devoted to teaching on spiritual deliverance?

Today, pastors, evangelists, and prophets teach on church growth, friendly evangelism, prosperity, and a host of other important subjects, but hardly ever do they mention deliverance. Don't get me wrong—I believe in teaching all those needed subjects. But why not devote a portion of those seminars to deliverance?

This de-emphasis on the devil and his demons is not only found in ecclesiastical and denominational churches; it also can be encountered in Pentecostal and charismatic churches, as well. Many in the Spirit-filled movement seem to be afraid to tackle the subject. Perhaps they don't want to be viewed as unscientific, or perhaps they are afraid that Christians will develop an unhealthy focus on demons. Whatever the case, I believe we need a new and greater emphasis on the need for deliverance, with a stress on biblical accuracy.

> *I believe we need a new and greater emphasis on the need for deliverance, with a stress on biblical accuracy.*

Is It the Devil?

I am often asked, "How can you tell if a sickness is caused by a demon or by natural causes?" This is a great question. After hours of research in Scripture, I have developed ways to determine whether or not demons are behind a sickness. For instance, I know that a sickness is demonic if:

1. The discerning of spirits is in operation

2. No natural cause of the illness can be determined

3. The disease becomes chronic when doctors had anticipated a full recovery

4. The sickness also affects the spiritual life of the afflicted

5. Strange occurrences accompany the illness.

6. The afflicted person becomes unusually ill or emotionally distraught in the presence of an anointed person

7. The afflicted person becomes homesick when he or she leaves town

8. The infirmity returns after the person has been spiritually healed

9. A more severe illness replaces the one from which the person was spiritually healed

10. The disease is hereditary, and it is discovered that the previous generation practiced idolatry

1. *The Discerning of Spirits Is in Operation*

*But to each one is given the manifestation of the Spirit to profit withal. For to one is given through the Spirit the word of wisdom; and to another the word of knowledge, according to the same Spirit: to another faith, in the same Spirit; and to another gifts of healings, in the one Spirit; and to another workings of miracles; and to another prophecy; and to another **discernings of spirits**; to another divers kinds of tongues; and to another the interpretation of tongues.*

(1 Corinthians 12:7–10 ASV, emphasis added)

Notice the seventh gift on the list: *"discernings of spirits."* God gives at times the ability to see and perceive the operations of both good and evil spirits. The Greek word for *discernings* comes from another Greek word meaning "to judge." At times, it is hard to judge whether or not a spirit is the cause of a sickness, but through the gifting of the Holy Spirit, believers have the ability to correctly perceive such matters.

The word *discernings* is plural because that is how it is in the original Greek. This means that discernment can come in various forms. Sometimes, it will come in the form of a vision in which you actually see the demon with your eyes.

One of the most influential charismatic leaders of our day, Kenneth Hagin, once told a story about a time when he was preaching in a country church and a man came forward for prayer. From his outward appearance, the man seemed normal, except that his face was grimaced in pain. As the man drew closer, Hagin experienced a vision. In this vision, he saw a monkey-like creature wrapping its arms around the man's head, as in a headlock. Immediately, Hagin exclaimed, "In the name of Jesus, you foul spirit, leave this man at once!"

The spirit looked startled that Hagin had actually seen it, then eyed him for a moment. Hagin stared right back and said, "I told you to leave this man."

The spirit, realizing it had been discovered, replied, "Well, I don't want to leave, but if you tell me to go, I have to go."

Hagin replied, "You will have to go."

The spirit let go of the man's head, jumped off his shoulders, and landed on the floor. Then, it looked at Hagin for a moment.

Hagin continued, "You will have to leave these premises, now." The spirit whimpered like a beaten dog and wobbled out of the church. Personally, I have not experienced such dramatic visions of demons, but I have had the *"discernings of spirits"* work in different ways.

The definition of *discern* is "to detect with the eyes; to detect with other senses than vision." As you can see from this definition, discernment is not perception by sight only, but can also come through the other senses: hearing, smell, taste, and touch.

Oral Roberts, one of the most famous healing evangelists, said that he could often smell the demon in a person. I'm pretty sure that no one else in the room with Roberts was able to smell anything, but he did. Others may claim that they *feel* the presence of a demon. They may start to sweat, get clammy, or have a tingling sensation. I have heard some say that they felt heat when they were in the presence of a demon. Kenneth Hagin was told by the Lord that whenever he laid both hands on the sick, if he felt fire going back and forth between his hands, there was the presence of a demon in the sick person he was praying for. Others may feel cold, a chill, or some other physical sensation. God is sovereign, and He will work with you in His way to help you discern the presence of demons.

In my experience, the most common way that discernment works is through a sense of "knowing"—an inner sense of confidence that a demon is there. You may call it intuition or a gut instinct, but you just "know that you know" that an evil spirit is at work behind the sickness.

2. No Natural Cause of the Illness Can Be Determined

A telltale sign that a demon may be inducing an illness is when there are no natural explanations for the sickness. This type of sickness is sometimes called *psychosomatic*. Some may believe that it's all in the afflicted person's head, that his or her mind is causing the symptoms. Many discount this kind of sickness. However, if the person is suffering pain or symptoms—even if you cannot pinpoint the cause—he or she is still hurting and in need of healing.

I believe that some of the cases that are labeled "psychosomatic illnesses" are actually caused by demons, and that this explains why doctors are sometimes unable to discover the cause. You cannot spot a demon on an X-ray; you cannot see a demon in a blood sample. Demons are not perceptible through scientific methods of investigation. In cases like this, I have found great success in bringing healing through deliverance. I have also found that the leading cause of psychosomatic illness is stress. (We will talk about stress in a later chapter.)

3. The Disease Becomes Chronic When Doctors Had Anticipated a Full Recovery

One of the great powers of the human body is its ability to heal itself. For example, when you cut yourself, the body immediately begins to heal the cut by sending bacteria-fighting agents to form a scab for protection. Eventually, the scab falls off, and the body is well. This is normal.

Consider what happens if an evil spirit is causing the infirmity. How can the body heal itself then? It can't. It simply won't be able to heal itself naturally if it is afflicted by an evil spirit.

Chronic illnesses are usually permanent. They stay with you. I believe that in some cases, chronic illnesses are demonic, and that is why they are permanent. No matter how hard the body tries to fight off a chronic illness, it can't because a demon is initiating the disease and not a natural occurrence. In cases like this, the demon must be driven out in order for healing to finally take place.

The Scripture at the beginning of this chapter deals with a woman who had *"a spirit of infirmity eighteen years, and was bent over"* (Luke 13:11 NKJV). It is unnatural for the human body to remain sick. If a bone breaks, it naturally heals. In this case, the woman's backbone had begun to form improperly. She had suffered for eighteen years. It was a chronic illness, and, according to the Bible, it was caused by a spirit. When it appears that a person should have recovered from an affliction but hasn't, I

> *It is unnatural for the human body to remain sick.*

deal with the evil spirit and drive it from the afflicted person.

4. The Sickness Also Affects the Spiritual Life of the Afflicted

Demons, when they are present, do not just affect the body physically; they also attack one's spiritual life. If the sick person feels peace even when he is sick, then the disease most likely is a natural one.

I often look for evidence of spiritual growth in the afflicted person's life. If it is evident, his disease is most likely from natural causes. On the other hand, if the afflicted person is also being attacked spiritually, there could be demonic roots of the illness. Demons are not interested in simply bringing physical infirmities, but they also desire to afflict the spiritual life.

One time, I was visiting a little church in the suburbs of Dallas. After preaching my heart out, I received little enthusiastic response from the congregation except for one dear old lady who kept shouting, "Praise the Lord. That's right! Keep preaching!" She was so exuberant.

After the service, while I was signing books, a gentleman walked up to me and said, "I want to apologize for my mother. She was the one who kept shouting, 'Praise the Lord.'" I told him that I had enjoyed her enthusiastic response. Then he said, "You see, she shouts praises because she has Alzheimer's." It seemed that the only person who liked my preaching that night was a lady with Alzheimer's.

Here is my point: this dear lady was afflicted, but she did not have a demon. A demon would never shout, "Praise the Lord!" Her disease was physical, not demonic. She was spiritually intact, even if her mind was diseased. On the other hand, I have seen sick people become furious at my preaching. Who would get furious over the preaching of the Word? Only the devil and his demons.

Many Christians are able to grow spiritually during times of sickness, proving that their afflictions are not demonic. In cases where the sick do not grow spiritually but instead become bitter, angry, and more sinful, I believe that their sicknesses have a demonic root. These people do not merely need physical healing; they need deliverance, as well.

> *Many Christians are able to grow spiritually during times of sickness, proving that their afflictions are not demonic.*

Give yourself a checkup. When you are physically sick, do you find yourself getting angry over studying Scripture, hearing the gospel preached, or even reading this book? If so, you may be sick not only in body but also in your spirit.

5. Strange Occurrences Accompany the Illness

A major sign that demons are causing an infirmity is the occurrence of strange things in the life of the infirmed. In the introduction, I mentioned Lori, who suffered from depression. How did she know it was a spirit that caused her depression? She knew it because she also had strange, unexplained marks on her body. She did not suffer just from clinical depression; there was something else tormenting her, and the marks on her body testified that supernatural agents were involved.

Here is a Scripture to consider:

When they came to the crowd, a man approached Jesus and knelt before him. "Lord, have mercy on my son," he said. "He has seizures and is suffering greatly. He often falls into the fire or into the water."... Jesus rebuked the demon, and it came out of the boy, and he was healed from that moment. (Matthew 17:14–15, 18)

How did Jesus recognize that the boy's problem wasn't simply an epileptic seizure? In this case, it may have been the fact that the seizures occurred at extremely inopportune times, during situations in which they endangered the boy's life. He had them around fire and water and fell into them. In my mind, that would qualify as a "strange occurrence" and a sign of the presence of demons.

This happens today, as well. I have successfully prayed deliverance for people who happen to become sick on Sunday mornings and at no other time. It seems clear in such cases that the devil is causing the infirmity to take place at specific times in order to keep the afflicted person from hearing the Word. Others may become sick whenever they begin to read the Bible or whenever they attempt to share their faith.

Someone might ask, "If a disease is diagnosed by doctors, doesn't that disprove a demonic cause?" Not necessarily. The Bible says, *"The body without the spirit is dead"* (James 2:26). Although you cannot see a person's spirit, it is the force that provides life for the body. Doctors may think that the heart keeps us alive, but Scripture tells us that it is the spirit. Likewise, there is a false assumption that no spirit can give life to a disease. On the contrary, just as there is an invisible force called a spirit that keeps our bodies alive, there are evil spirits that can breathe life into diseases.

> *Just as there is an invisible force called a spirit that keeps our bodies alive, there are evil spirits that can breathe life into diseases.*

Once the evil spirit is cast out of the body, however, the

disease—left alone without its life source—must die. This is why a disease may have both physical and demonic roots.

6. The Afflicted Person Becomes Unusually Ill or Emotionally Distraught in the Presence of an Anointed Person

So they brought him. When the spirit saw Jesus, it immediately threw the boy into a convulsion. He fell to the ground and rolled around, foaming at the mouth. (Mark 9:20)

In Mark's account of the epileptic boy, notice that the convulsions began as soon as the spirit was in the presence of Jesus. I have seen people become physically and emotionally ill the moment they are in my presence. They can't understand it. Some become nauseated, grow depressed, or experience intense fear. They refuse prayer or feel agitated when others pray for them. They may be seriously ill, but instead of turning to a minister to pray for them, they often despise the minister. This is a clear sign that demons are involved with those people.

Another related symptom is when mentally ill people become angry or nervous around me. I have heard people scream during church services. They say, "I want to leave! Get me out of here!" The anointing on me seems to torment the demons inside of them. This is what happened in the case of the epileptic boy and Jesus. The demon threw the boy to the ground as soon as it saw Jesus.

A person may fall to the ground in God's presence because of His power and holiness or because of an evil spirit. You can tell the difference by observing the person's behavior when he is on the ground. Does he look peaceful and joyful? Or, is he writhing, growling, and screaming? Unfortunately, many Christians do not have the discernment to tell the difference.

These signs should be obvious that demons are present and causing people to act in bizarre ways. Yet, many ministers leave people alone and attribute these weird acts to the Holy Spirit. We need to obey Scripture, which says, *"Test the spirits to see whether they are from God"* (1 John 4:1).

7. *The Afflicted Person Becomes Homesick When He or She Leaves Town*

Jesus had said to him, "Come out of this man, you evil spirit!" Then Jesus asked him, "What is your name?" "My name is Legion," he replied, "for we are many." And he begged Jesus again and again not to send them out of the area. (Mark 5:8–10)

The demon *"begged"* Jesus not to send him *"out of the area."* For some reason, demons prefer to stay in the same location, if possible. One reason may have something to do with rank and territory. The apostle Paul lists four ranks of evil spiritual entities in Ephesians: rulers, authorities, powers, and forces. (See Ephesians 6:12.) It appears that demons must answer to higher-ranking demons. It could be that they do not want to leave the area without proper demonic authority because it might seem as though they went AWOL. Perhaps they do not want to be disciplined by a higher-ranking spirit. This is only my speculation, but it seems certain that demons are reticent to leave their particular territories.

> *Since demons prefer to stay in certain locations, the demonically sick may find themselves unwilling to venture away from their homes or cities.*

This brings us to another sign of demonic activity in the sick. Since demons prefer to stay in certain locations, the demonically sick may find themselves unwilling to venture away from their homes or cities. When they do leave, they may become homesick and wish to return.

Many sick people who are afraid of leaving their houses may have demons. Doctors call this affliction *agoraphobia*. It is not normal to want to remain at home all the time. We are social creatures who need to get out and be with other people, or even to leave town for periods of time. This is normal, healthy behavior.

People who suffer from forms of demonic sickness may turn down lucrative employment opportunities because they don't want to leave their homes or cities. Of course, many people stay in one place because they have family nearby and a good church, in which case their desire is understandable. But some people have no legitimate reasons for turning down promotions or educational opportunities except for the fact that they are troubled with sickness. This is a sign of demonic infirmities.

8. *The Infirmity Returns after the Person Has Been Spiritually Healed*

When an evil spirit comes out of a man, it goes through arid places seeking rest and does not find it. Then it says, "I will return to the house I left." When it arrives, it finds the house unoccupied, swept clean and put in order. Then it goes and takes with it seven other spirits more wicked than itself, and they go in and live there. And the final condition of that man is worse than the first. That is how it will be with this wicked generation. (Matthew 12:43–45)

Jesus taught that demons may try to come back to a person after being cast out. One sign that a disease has demonic origins is when it *returns*. When a person has been naturally healed, the disease is unlikely to return. The odds are extremely low. However, demons will try to return, bringing with them the disease from which the person had been healed. When this occurs, I usually look for the demon behind the disease and cast it out.

9. A More Severe Illness Replaces the One from Which the Person Was Spiritually Healed

Jesus said, *"And the final condition of that man is worse than the first"* (Matthew 12:45).

There are people who get healed from one condition only to get sick later with something worse. They might even get better from that disease, but then an even more severe disease comes on them. Something is desperately wrong in these cases. Some people seem never able to stay well. It should be obvious that something supernatural is taking place, and that the afflicted person should definitely seek deliverance.

10. The Disease Is Hereditary, and It Is Discovered That the Previous Generation Practiced Idolatry

In the next chapter we will discuss hereditary diseases. If it can be proven that a previous generation of the afflicted person's family practiced idolatry, then demons may be causing the disease.

Seek God

These are some of the ways to judge whether a physical disease is the result of demons or of natural causes. You do not necessarily have to experience everything I mentioned in this chapter, but if you or someone you know has one of these symptoms, take the matter to God in prayer.

Only God is authorized to show you whether or not you have a *"spirit of infirmity"* (Luke 13:11 KJV). If He confirms it, keep reading—help is on the way!

Chapter Two

Generational Curses

Mary had just returned from a visit to the doctor, who had confirmed her suspicions and fears. "I'm sorry to tell you this," he'd said, "but the cyst is cancerous." In her heart, she had known it before the doctor had said the words. Cancer ran in her family. Her mother had died of it, her older sister, Sofia, was being treated for it, and now it was her turn.

It isn't fair! Mary lamented. *Other women are never going to get cancer simply because they had different parents.* Mary's situation is similar to many other people's experiences.

Hereditary diseases are common. Research is proving that genetics play a major role in one's health—or the lack thereof. Does it seem unfair that one should inherit the trait of disease from one's parents? Actually, the idea of inheriting blessings and curses from our parents is seen throughout Scripture. Consider the most far-reaching generational curse ever to come upon the human race—the one that came from Adam.

> *For just as through the disobedience of the one man the many were made sinners, so also through the obedience of the one man the many will be made righteous.*
>
> (Romans 5:19)

We inherited our sin nature from Adam. We may not like it, but it is true nevertheless. Consequently, we suffer under the same curse that befell Adam. This would not be fair if God had not made provision for us to be free from the curses of our ancestors. But He did. Jesus is the answer.

> *The cross redeems us from any curse that tries to attach itself to us.*

Consider the cross. It is both vertical and horizontal. The vertical aspect speaks of our relationship with God. The horizontal aspect speaks of our relationships with other people. The cross redeems us from any curse that tries to attach itself to us. Whether the curse is judgment from God or a result of the sin of others, Christ has *"redeemed us from the curse"* (Galatians 3:13 KJV).

Sin brings a curse. It's that simple! Read Deuteronomy 28. Here, God warned Israel that if they should sin and break His commandments, they would be under a curse.

However, if you do not obey the LORD your God and do not carefully follow all his commands and decrees I am giving you today, all these curses will come upon you and overtake you: You will be cursed in the city and cursed in the country. Your basket and your kneading trough will be cursed. The fruit of your womb will be cursed, and the crops of your land, and the calves of your herds and the lambs of your flocks. You will be cursed when you come in and cursed when you go out. (Deuteronomy 28:15–19)

Notice how often God mentions the word *"cursed."* The whole concept of a curse can sound superstitious to the modern mind. Some think that curses do not exist, but they do! However, curses do not come without reason. *"Like a fluttering sparrow or a darting swallow, an undeserved curse does not come to rest"* (Proverbs 26:2). Curses must be deserved, for they will not rest on just anyone. The King James Version puts the passage in these words: *"As the bird by wandering, as the swallow by flying, so the curse causeless shall not come."* A *"curse causeless shall not come"* to rest. In other words, there must be a cause or reason for the curse. And, as I mentioned before, the reason for curses is sin.

Idolatry

There is one particular sin that is very offensive to God and extremely dangerous to your life and the lives of your children. What sin is that? It is a violation of the second of the Ten Commandments:

> *You shall not make for yourself an idol in the form of anything in heaven above or on the earth beneath or in the waters below. You shall not bow down to them or worship them; for I, the LORD your God, am a jealous God, punishing the children for the sin of the fathers to the third and fourth generation of those who hate me, but showing love to a thousand generations of those who love me and keep my commandments.*
>
> (Exodus 20:4–6)

Breaking the second commandment is so offensive to God that it brings a curse on the offender and his children until the fourth generation. None of the other Ten Commandments has this curse. Why this one? Why is the sin of idolatry so heinous that there is a curse placed on the individual and his posterity?

First of all, what is idolatry? It is worshipping idols. An idol is a representative—the image or likeness—of some god. Question: Is there more than one God? Of course not; there is only one God. Then, what are these so-called gods? Paul provided the answer in 1 Corinthians 10:19–20:

> *Do I mean then that a sacrifice offered to an idol is anything, or that an idol is anything?*

No, but the sacrifices of pagans are offered to demons, not to God, and I do not want you to be participants with demons.

Paul told us that an idol is nothing. It is really not a god, nor does it represent a true god. Then, he made a startling revelation: an idol is a demon. This is very important to understand. When a person worships or pays homage to an idol, he is actually worshipping a demon. He may not be aware that he is worshiping demons, but he is, nevertheless.

> **When a person worships or pays homage to an idol, he is actually worshipping a demon.**

Paul did not pull this revelation out of a hat. He received it from the Hebrew Scriptures:

They made him jealous with their foreign gods and angered him with their detestable idols. They sacrificed to demons, which are not God—gods they had not known, gods that recently appeared, gods your fathers did not fear.　　(Deuteronomy 32:16–17)

There it is—idols are demons.

Since we have discovered that idols are demons, how does this relate to a curse being placed on the idolater's family? To answer this, we must go to the New Testament and look at the teachings that Jesus gave concerning demons.

When an evil spirit comes out of a man, it goes through arid places seeking rest and does not find it. Then it says, "I will return to the house I left." When it arrives, it finds the house unoccupied, swept clean and put in order. Then it goes and takes with it seven other spirits more wicked than itself, and they go in and live there. And the final condition of that man is worse than the first. That is how it will be with this wicked generation. (Matthew 12:43–45)

According to Jesus, when a demon leaves a person, it tries to come back and bring with it other spirits worse than itself. Then Jesus said, *"That is how it will be with this wicked generation."*

The Greek word for *"generation"* is *genea*, from which we get our word *gene*. Jesus was telling some of the people of His day that their genes came from wicked parents who had worshipped demons. Those demons were still in those families and had brought even more evil spirits with them. As a result, some of them had grown even more wicked than their parents had been.

When a demon-possessed person dies, what happens to the demon? Is it buried with

> *When an evil spirit is invited into a person's life through idolatry, that spirit can continue to follow the genealogical line.*

the deceased? Of course not! It is very possible that the demon simply moves on to the children. This is how the generational curse works. When an evil spirit is invited into a person's life through idolatry, that spirit can continue to follow the genealogical line. This explains how children may be afflicted by their parents' sin.

Another proof that demons stay within a family is found in a term used for demons. A common Old Testament designation for demons is *"familiar spirits"* (Deuteronomy 18:11 KJV). In Spanish, the word for *family* is *familia*, which is similar to this word. The Hebrew word is *'owb*, which conveys the same thought. As you can see, a familiar spirit can also be a "family" spirit.

Greed

Most people from educated backgrounds feel a sense of security. They can't imagine anyone in their family ever committing idolatry. However, there is another form of idolatry that many people, especially educated ones, commit. The form of idolatry I am talking about is greed. *"For of this you can be sure: No immoral, impure or greedy person—such a man is an idolater—has any inheritance in the kingdom of Christ and of God"* (Ephesians 5:5).

Who is an idolater? A *"greedy person—such a man is an idolater."* Wow! Most people think of idolaters as isolated pagans in poor countries who practice voodoo. They never imagine that an idolater may be a member of the stock exchange living in Manhattan. However, the Word of God expands our understanding of idolatry. It includes every segment of society—from the obvious idolaters to the not-so-obvious. There is both *overt* idolatry and *covert* idolatry. Regardless of which category one's idolatry falls under, it is still idolatry.

Greed brings a curse down on your children. Look at 2 Peter 2:14: *"With eyes full of adultery, they never stop sinning; they seduce the unstable; they are experts in greed—an accursed brood!"*

The *"accursed brood"* are experts in greed. The word *brood* is rather outdated. We do not use it often. Of course, Jesus also called the religious leaders a *"brood of vipers"* (Matthew 12:34).

The King James Version says they are a *"generation of vipers"* (2 Peter 2:14). A cursed child has bad blood.

Modern medicine has discovered the relationship between genetics and health. It is often possible to predict whether a child is likely to become ill based on the health of the parents. The blood of each individual contains his or her genetic makeup. We inherit our genes from our parents. If their blood is cursed, then we often inherit their cursed genes.

We see this in the life of Gehazi, the apprentice prophet of Elisha. Elisha had just finished healing Naaman. Naaman offered money to Elisha, but he turned it down. Elisha wanted to make a big impact on this pagan officer, so he did not want money to get in the way of converting him and the nation he served.

Gehazi, however, felt differently. He said to himself, *My master let this man off too easily.* Then Gehazi went after Naaman and lied, saying that Elisha would take some money for his friends who had come to visit. Gehazi then hid the money in his tent.

> *Then* [Gehazi] *went in and stood before his master Elisha. "Where have you been, Gehazi?" Elisha asked. "Your servant didn't go anywhere," Gehazi answered. But Elisha said to him, "Was not my spirit with you when the man got down from his chariot to meet you? Is this the time to take money, or to accept clothes, olive groves, vineyards, flocks, herds, or menservants and maidservants? Naaman's leprosy will cling to you and to your descendants forever." Then Gehazi went from Elisha's presence and he was leprous, as white as snow.* (2 Kings 5:25–27)

It is clear that Gehazi was greedy, but notice his punishment: he inherited Naaman's leprosy, and his children did, as well. Gehazi operated in greed, which is idolatry. Idolatry opens us to demons, and demons like to stay in the family. Gehazi's children inherited demons. Through the demons came the generational curses.

Chapter Three

How to Break Generational Curses

You would probably consider it unfair to be judged for your parents' sin. The fact is, God will *not* judge you for your parents' sin. When He spelled out the Ten Commandments, God said, *"I, the LORD your God, am a jealous God, punishing the children for the sin of the fathers to the third and fourth generation of those who hate me"* (Exodus 20:5). God is not just picking on the children of sinners but on the children of those who hate God.

Those who love God but are in sin are accountable for their own actions, as God confirms in Ezekiel: *"For every living soul belongs to me, the father as well as the son—both alike belong to me. The soul who sins is the one who will die"* (Ezekiel 18:4).

The child of one who sins is not held responsible for the father's actions. To drive this point home, Ezekiel includes the following illustration about a sinful father and a righteous son:

> But suppose this son has a son who sees all the sins his father commits, and though he sees them, he does not do such things.... He will not die for his father's sin; he will surely live....Yet you ask, "Why does the son not share the guilt of his father?" Since the son has done what is just and right and has been careful to keep all my decrees, he will surely live. The soul who sins is the one who will die. The son will not share the guilt of the father, nor will the father share the guilt of the son.
>
> (Ezekiel 18:14, 17, 19–20)

A generational curse is not automatic; it can be broken! It does not have to be a permanent situation.

Ezekiel was not contradicting what God said in Exodus about punishing future generations of children, because God said He would punish only *"those who hate me."* In other words, punishment came only to those who continued in the same disobedient path of their parents. Therefore, a generational curse is not automatic; it can be broken! It does not have to be a permanent situation.

Unfortunately, experience tells us that children often follow the life patterns of their parents. It is common to see many hurtful life choices passed down, such as addiction, obesity, teen pregnancy, worry, anger, abuse, divorce, gambling, laziness, adultery, crime, and so many other sinful behaviors. The Bible gives several examples of sons following in the missteps of their fathers.

Consider Abraham and Isaac. Abraham gave his wife, Sarah, to Pharaoh for fear of losing his life. (See Genesis 12:10–20.) His son, Isaac, did exactly the same thing when confronted with fear. He gave his wife, Rebekah, to King Abimelech, just like his daddy did. (See Genesis 26:7.) Children often inherit their parents' destructive habits.

As I was teaching this to a group of prisoners, I asked for a show of hands of the men who were simply repeating the awful things they had seen in the life of at least one of their parents. Out of the seventy men present, sixty-five raised their hands. Only five admitted to being the prodigal sons who had abandoned the godly lifestyles of their fathers. By far, the majority of men in prison are not the black sheep of the family but only representatives of their families' dysfunction. Children will not escape generational curses if they continue in the ways of their parents. We are fooling ourselves if we expect our curses to be broken, yet we do not want to repent.

Curses come in many forms. According to Deuteronomy 28,

If you fully obey the LORD your God and carefully follow all his commands I give you today, the LORD your God will set you high above all the nations on earth. All these blessings will come upon you and accompany you if you obey the LORD your God: You will be blessed in the city and blessed in the country. The fruit of your womb will be blessed, and the crops of your land and the young of your livestock—the calves of your herds and the lambs of your flocks.

(verses 1–4)

Those under a curse will experience failure and calamity in their lives. They may experience chronic or life-threatening diseases, such as diabetes and cancer. Mental illnesses, including thoughts of suicide, may haunt them. They may be plagued by marital conflict. Their children may fall into various forms of bondage. They may exist in a state of continual financial lack. If you are experiencing some of these effects, you might be under a curse, but only the Holy Spirit can make the proper diagnosis. If your parents suffered under similar circumstances and hardship, then it is likely that you are under a generational curse. In such cases, you may need to deal with the presence of demons.

Making Reparations

In order to break a curse, you need to understand whether or not the curse originated with you or with your parents, grandparents, or great-grandparents. If it originated with them, then, believe it or not, you need to confess the sins of your relatives. It is essential—and even scriptural—to confess the sins of

It is essential—and even scriptural—to confess the sins of previous generations.

previous generations. Look at this example from Nehemiah's life:

> *Then I said: "O LORD, God of heaven, the great and awesome God, who keeps his covenant of love with those who love him and obey his commands, let your ear be attentive and your eyes open to hear the prayer your servant is praying before you day and night for your servants, the people of Israel. I confess the sins we Israelites, including myself and my father's house, have committed against you."*
>
> (Nehemiah 1:5–6)

Nehemiah confessed not only his sins but also the sins of his *"father's house."* He went back to the past to make things right.

You may wonder, *Is this really necessary?* I believe that if we ignore the past, we are liable to repeat it. If we do not get brutally honest about our forefathers' sins, then we are apt to fall into them ourselves. Research has shown that the reason it is hard for children to break free from the patterns set by their parents is that they either try to hide their parents' lifestyle or they simply deny it. Secrecy and denial are the chief culprits of continuing generational curses.

The Bible says to establish everything by two or three witnesses. (See 2 Corinthians 13:1.) Consider the words of the prophet Jeremiah: *"O LORD, we acknowledge our wickedness and the guilt of **our fathers**; we have indeed sinned against you"* (Jeremiah 14:20, emphasis added). Notice his need to confess *"the guilt of our fathers"* in order not to follow in the same footsteps. I would take this a step further. Not only must we confess and repent from our fathers' sins; we must also, if possible, make reparations for the damage they created by those sins.

Let's say, for example, that your father was a racist. It is not good enough to simply abstain from making racist remarks yourself. You need to be about the work of racial reconciliation by actually seeking to establish harmony between different race groups. You need to do the exact opposite of what your father did. That is true repentance.

In my case, my father was abusive to my mother. He was a bar owner who drank heavily.

He never took us on family vacations. In fact, he rarely spent time with us at all.

My mother was not the best parental example herself, especially when I was an infant. Refusing to give up her party lifestyle, she essentially handed off her children to my father's mother—my grandmother—to raise. My sister and I never witnessed a good example of a mother or a father. On top of that, my grandmother and grandfather were not kind to each other while we lived with them. They even slept in separate bedrooms.

> *Without the strong hand of the Lord in my life, I was destined to continue the pattern set by my parents and their parents.*

Therefore, I grew up under a generational curse. This is probably why I feel so strongly about breaking generational curses. Without the strong hand of the Lord in my life, I was destined to continue the pattern set by my parents and their parents. Thankfully, I came to the Lord and understood clearly that this string of dysfunction had to end with me, or else my children would be doomed to fall into the same ways.

I made a conscious effort not only to repent for my father and mother's sins, but also to make a strong stand against their lifestyle. For example, when a wife tells me that her husband has abused her, I counsel her that, based on Scripture, she is permitted to leave her husband.

"'I hate divorce,' says the LORD God of Israel, 'and I hate a man's covering himself with violence'" (Malachi 2:16). The Lord is disgusted with both divorce and domestic violence. A husband cannot expect his wife to remain in the marriage if he beats her. When a husband abuses his wife, it is equal to divorce. Therefore, I do not feel that a woman is constrained to remain in such a relationship. I do not advocate "easy divorce," but no wife should feel any religious obligation to live in the fear and hurt of an abusive marriage.

When I meet with abusive husbands in my office, they get a tongue-lashing that they won't soon forget. Why? I feel that it is my duty to reverse the type of damage that my father helped to create in my family and in other families, as well.

I am the same way with drunkenness. I saw my father come home from the bar drunk nearly every night. Since getting married and having children of my own, I have committed to never become intoxicated. My children will never be able to say that they saw their daddy drunk—not even once.

To counter family neglect, I take my family on vacations as often as possible, usually two or three times a year. I never intend to fall into the same neglectful patterns that I saw in my father. As difficult as raising children may be, I have tried to give my children my time—the very thing I did not experience growing up. I am far from the perfect dad, but I know the importance of making a diligent effort to truly abandon the sins of the past generation. I believe God has honored my effort, and, for the most part, I have experienced blessings instead of curses.

Today, I can happily say that my father knows the Lord. I was privileged to baptize him in water as one of the first members of my church. Rarely did he miss a service while he was healthy. My mother was saved before me and was instrumental in bringing me to the Lord. She continues to be a devoted wife, mother, and grandmother. What a turnaround! She has become a tremendous blessing and a great example. The generational curse in our family's life has truly been broken!

Clean House

Your family's curses can be broken, too. Confess your family's sin, right now. Say:

In the name of Jesus, I confess my sins and the sins of my ancestors. I confess [name some of the sins, being as specific as you can]. I refuse to allow the past to determine my future. I renounce and reject all past sins. To the best of my ability, I will work to make things right.

Next, you need to rid your home of any idolatrous objects that may have been passed on to you: statues, beads, relics, crystals, luck charms, paintings, and so forth. You do not need to get rid of gifts from your parents or grandparents that have had no association with idolatry. You may also need to get rid of—or return to the original owners—any "blood money." This would include money won from gambling, stolen objects, or profits from illegal or immoral activities.

After ridding your house of these objects, you need to claim your inheritance in Christ. Although your blood may be tainted, the blood of Jesus will cleanse you from all sin. You need to believe more in the power of Jesus' blood than in the power of your ancestors' blood.

> *You need to believe more in the power of Jesus' blood than in the power of your ancestors' blood.*

Release yourself from the curse through prayer. You must bless your home and your family by speaking God's blessings over your lives. You may want to use a prayer like this:

In the name of Jesus, I declare that I am a child of God. The blood of Jesus has regenerated me. I do not have to live under any curse. Christ has redeemed me from the curse of the law. I take my authority as a child of God, and I release my grandchildren, my children, and myself from all generational curses. I command every demon to leave my bloodline, right now! By Jesus' stripes, we are healed and blessed!

At this point, you may be wondering whether or not your prayer worked. You must not doubt. *"The prayer of a righteous man* [or woman] *is powerful and effective"* (James 5:16). Don't allow doubt or fear to infect your prayers. Stand in faith and believe that the demons have left you and your family.

Instead of repeating this prayer over and over again, pray a prayer of thanksgiving. Thank God that you are free.

I thank You, Father, that I am free from the generational curse. I do not inherit anything from my parents or grandparents. I am a new creation in Christ Jesus. Old things are passed away, and all things are new. I live under the new covenant with better blessings. I am blessed in the city and blessed in the country. Everything I set my hands to do is blessed. My children are blessed, too. I am the head and not the tail, above only and not beneath.

Chapter Four

Redeemed from the Curses

Isabella phoned, crying, "Pastor Brown, you do not know me, but I have watched several of your videos online, and I feel that you are the person who can help me."

"How may I help you?" I asked.

"I have many curses put on me by many people. I am under a generational curse. On top of that, a coworker who is into witchcraft told me that she put a curse on me. Ever since I can remember, I have been cursed. I am constantly sick. I never have money to do anything. I am at the end of myself. Please help me."

I asked her if she was saved, and she quickly affirmed, "Oh, I have been saved since I was twelve. I love the Lord."

I probed her mind. "Isabella, are you familiar with Galatians three, verse thirteen? It says, *'Christ redeemed us from the curse of the law by becoming a curse for us.'"*

She paused for a moment. "Yes, I have heard that verse before," she said.

"Isabella, tell me what the verse means to you."

She fumbled through an inadequate explanation. "I guess it has something to do with Jesus dying for me. Maybe it means I will go to heaven when I die."

"Is that all?"

"I don't know anything beyond that."

I proceeded to explain to her what I am going to explain in this chapter. Isabella was like many of the people who have called me asking to be freed from their curses. Surprisingly, many have been Christians for years yet do not have a revelation of their redemption from curses. They always give their curses such power, yet the Bible says, *"Christ redeemed us from the curse."* Is Christ's work greater than the work of any generational curse? Is His work greater than any curse that someone has tried to place on you? Of course it is. Yet, many misinformed saints put too much stock in the curses and not enough confidence in the finished work of the cross.

> *Many misinformed saints put too much stock in the curses and not enough confidence in the finished work of the cross.*

What Is Redemption?

A curse is an invisible force intended to bring judgment, harm, and misfortune to another. I do not discount the reality of the power of curses. You may be crying out like Isabella, "I'm born again. I love You, Lord, but nothing seems to be working for me. I can't pay my bills, I can't control my children, my spouse doesn't love me, I'm depressed all the time, and I am always struggling with sickness and pain." The only explanation is that you must be under a curse.

Curses are real, but so is Christ's redemption.

The Greek word for *redemption* is *eksagorazo,* meaning "by payment of a price to recover from the power of another, to ransom." It suggests that a previous owner owned an object but lost it through debt, only to purchase it back.

Isaiah supports this concept.

*This is what the L*ORD *says: "Where is your mother's certificate of divorce with which I sent her away? Or to which of my creditors did I sell you? Because of your sins you were sold; because of your transgressions your mother was sent away."* (Isaiah 50:1)

You are probably familiar with the concept of repossession. A creditor regains possession of an item because of nonpayment by the purchaser. The only way for the purchaser to get the item back is to pay what is owed, usually with interest. In pawn shops, when a person sells an item, he is usually given a "redemption ticket." This ticket gives him the right to buy back what he sold, but interest is added to the bill. The only one who can have a redemption ticket is the previous owner. Anyone else interested in buying the item has to pay much more.

In our case, we are not the owner. God is. Therefore, He is the only One who has the right to redeem us. We cannot redeem ourselves, even though it was our own sin that sold us into slavery. Even if we had the right to redeem ourselves, we do not have the righteousness necessary to afford the price that will free us from sin.

> *Obedience alone cannot provide the confidence you need to claim freedom from curses. The only sure confidence is the blood of Christ.*

You may hear someone suggest that you can redeem yourself through vigilant obedience, but that is unscriptural. While it is always beneficial in keeping the door closed on the devil, obedience alone cannot provide the confidence you need to claim freedom from curses. The only sure confidence is the blood of Christ.

For you know that it was not with perishable things such as silver or gold that you were redeemed from the empty way of life handed down to you from your forefathers, but with the precious blood of Christ, a lamb without blemish or defect.

(1 Peter 1:18–19)

Everything else is worthless. Your promise to change your ways is of no value; the deals you make with God are useless. Our sins have us so far in debt that we have no hope of ever paying off what we owe. We need to have confidence in the blood of Christ.

How can one man pay for the sins of the entire world? It is because this one man is the Creator. The Creator is always greater than the creation. *"Be shepherds of the church of God, which he bought with his own blood"* (Acts 20:28). This verse equates Jesus' blood with God's blood. This means that Jesus' blood is much greater than the life of every person. Only God can redeem us by His blood, and Jesus did it.

The Curse of the Law

"Christ redeemed us from the curse of the law" (Galatians 3:13). Many know that Christ redeemed them from *sin*, but only a few know that He also redeemed them from *"the curse of the law."*

The apostle Paul was referring to the curse uttered at Mount Ebal. Moses instructed the Israelites that when they entered into the Promised Land, they were to send six tribes to the top of Mount Gerizim to proclaim blessings for obedience to the laws of God and six tribes to the top of Mount Ebal to proclaim curses for disobedience to the laws of God. (See Deuteronomy 27:11–26.) We know Paul had this historical event in the life of Israel in mind because he wrote, *"All who rely on observing the law are under a curse, for it is written: 'Cursed is everyone who does not continue to do everything written in the Book of the Law'"* (Galatians 3:10). This was a quote from the passage in Deuteronomy in which the priests recited the curses: *"Cursed is the man who does not uphold the words of this law by carrying them out"* (Deuteronomy 27:26). This is the last verse before Deuteronomy 28, which lists all the specific and varied curses for all who disobeyed the law. The curses included fevers, inflammation, painful boils, and illness. They also included financial lack, failed crops, lost wages, increased and crushing debt, and utter poverty. Other descriptions of the curses included mental illness and confusion, constant fear and stress, marital failures, and spousal adultery. (See Deuteronomy 28.)

The good news is that Christ redeemed you not just from hell, but also from this curse of the law.

The good news is that Christ redeemed you not just from hell, but also from this curse of the law.

Now, if Christ redeemed you from all these curses,

why would you continue to carry them? There is no reason you should still be battling curses. You need to stand against them based on your covenant right. Take some time to read through Deuteronomy 28. Then, realize that you are redeemed from each and every curse mentioned. Praise God!

Some will argue that the phrase *"curse of the law"* (Galatians 3:13) is singular, as opposed to the plural *curses*, and therefore is not a reference to all the curses in Deuteronomy 28. They suggest that Paul was talking about one curse in particular.

The confusion stems from the failure to recognize that the word *curse* is a reference to the declaration made on Mount Ebal. It is the pronouncement of judgment for disobeying the law. With the pronouncement come the actual curses. If you are redeemed from the *curse of the law,* then you are redeemed from the *curses of the law,* as well. The people who misunderstand are reading the passage as though Christ has redeemed us from the "cursed law." In other words, they say it is the law that Christ redeemed us from, and not the negative consequences of disobeying the law. However, this interpretation makes the law itself the cause of the curse. It is not being under the law that brings a curse; rather, it is disobeying the law (by committing sin) that brings a curse.

On the other hand, the law also declares blessings for those who obey it. Paul made this abundantly clear. *"What shall we say, then? Is the law sin? Certainly not!"* (Romans 7:7). Later he reaffirmed the goodness of the law: *"So then, the law is holy, and the commandment is holy, righteous and good"* (verse 12).

The error people make as a result of misinterpreting this passage is teaching that the law is a cursed thing in and of itself. They are actually calling the law "cursed." This is blasphemous.

While it is true that we, as Christians, are not under the Mosaic law, we can claim the blessings of the law as though we had obeyed it because the blessing given to Abraham is ours. Paul explained the ramifications of being redeemed from the curse of the law: *"He redeemed us in order that the blessing given to Abraham might come to the Gentiles through Christ Jesus, so that by faith we might receive the promise of the Spirit"* (Galatians 3:14).

The reason for redemption is so that we might have *"the blessing given to Abraham."* The Bible says, *"The LORD had blessed [Abraham] in every way"* (Genesis 24:1). He was blessed with a long, healthy life. He was incredibly wealthy and sound in mind and emotions. His marriage was strong. There was no lack in Abraham's life. That is the way you are to be blessed. The opposite of a curse is a blessing. Instead of focusing on the curses in your life, you need to claim the blessings that are rightfully yours.

As I shared this with Isabella, she began to weep with joy. She was discovering the power of the blessing she was under. You are under that same blessing. Yet, if your focus is on the curses—the bad things that happen to you—your fear will continue to usher them in and reinforce the effects of sin in your life.

What Are You Relying On?

"All who rely on observing the law are under a curse, for it is written: 'Cursed is everyone who does not continue to do everything written in the Book of the Law'" (Galatians 3:10). The issue is what you *"rely on."* Are you relying on perfect obedience? Are you relying on the perfect obedience of your parents? Are you relying on the obedience of others? If you are, then you are *"under a curse."* No one is putting a curse on you; you are putting yourself under a curse. You do so through your confidence in the flesh. You need to start having confidence in God alone.

Suppose you get a traffic ticket that requires you to pay a hundred-dollar fine. A friend with more money than you says, "I will pay the ticket." Your friend writes a hundred-dollar check to the court for you to pay your fine. Do you then rush to your bank and ask if you have enough money to cover the traffic ticket? Of course not, because the money for the ticket is not coming out of your account but out of the account of your friend. Are you afraid to use the check because your parents have no money? Of course not, because any money your parents have or don't have is irrelevant in paying the ticket. As long as your friend has the money, no one's poverty can stop that check from cashing. The only hindrance will be if you are afraid to use the check to pay the ticket.

This is what people have done with the curses. They believe more in the poverty of their parents, or in the curse put on them by some acquaintance or stranger, than in the wealth God has bestowed upon them. God has redeemed you. You need to rely on Him to turn your curses into blessings.

Claim Your Rights

But when the time had fully come, God sent his Son, born of a woman, born under law, to redeem those under law, that we might receive the full **rights** *of sons.*
(Galatians 4:4–5, emphasis added)

God redeemed us so that *"we might receive the full rights of sons."* It is your *right* to be healed of every disease. It is your *right* to be financially blessed. It is your *right* to be emotionally whole. But your healing must be claimed; you cannot allow the enemy to steal what belongs to you.

God told Joshua, *"I will give you every place where you set your foot"* (Joshua 1:3). God gives only those places where we stomp our feet and say, "This piece of land is mine!" You must declare out loud to the devil that you will not stay sick, broke, and defeated.

As I shared this with Isabella, she began to shout in victory that she was blessed. Instantly the fear left her. The pain she'd felt was gone!

You need to look at healing not as a special gift but rather as your right. I know that this is a new concept to many people. Most people pray to God for a special *gift* of healing rather than see health as their God-given, blood-bought right. If

> *You need to look at healing not as a special gift but rather as your right.*

you went to baggage claim at the airport to get your luggage and saw someone pick up your suitcase to steal it, what would you do? You would not politely request, "Please, out of the kindness of your heart, would you give me my suitcase?" No, you would hold out your hand and say, "Hey, buddy! That's my suitcase. Drop it." If the thief argued, you would call security and show them your baggage claim ticket. You would fight to retrieve your luggage. Why? Because the luggage belongs to you; it is your right to have it.

The same is true of health. You cannot see health simply as a gift that God may or may not give you. You must see that He purchased health for you. He wants you to have it if you will just cash in on your redemption.

Terry Rubeiro is a deacon of my church. After he had triple bypass surgery on his heart, fear gripped him. He had difficulty leaving his house, afraid that he would suffer another heart attack. His attendance at church suffered. It was a difficult time in his life; however, he had built a big enough reserve of knowledge of the Word of God through the years that it kept him from utter despair.

He had heard me say over and over again that Jesus redeemed us from sickness. Regrettably, those had been just words to Terry. But as he began to meditate on all the previous teachings of redemption, those words took on a brand-new revelation. They entered deep into his heart, and joy came forth. He realized that he was truly healed and redeemed. His attendance at church bounced back. I saw a new joy in him. The difference was a revelation of his redemption.

After about two years, his wife, Colleen, encouraged him to get a cardiogram to see how he was doing. At first, he did not want to take the test due to the nagging fear that the doctors would find something wrong, but he quickly replaced that thought with faith and submitted to the test.

A few days later, they called him and asked if he could come back and retake the test. He asked, "Is there something wrong?"

"Oh, no," they said, "there is nothing to alarm you. There are some strange anomalies with the tests, and we simply want you to retake it at our expense."

So, Terry went back to retake the test. After several more tests, the doctors said, "Mr. Rubeiro, we have never seen anything like this before. But the tests show that you did not even have surgery. The arteries in your leg have grown back. The blood pumping to your heart is not from the replaced arteries but from brand-new, thick ones. It's amazing! After looking at these tests, if we did not know better, we would not even believe you had open-heart surgery. You are totally healthy." The doctors even had Terry speak to the medical field about his healing.

The key for Terry was his revelation. He laid claim to what was already his. Of course, you cannot lay claim to anything from God unless you are sure God has provided the blessing for you. I have discovered that a great many Christians find it difficult to have faith in divine healing. It is my goal in the next chapter to remove any lingering doubts you might have concerning healing.

Chapter Five

Healing in the Atonement

There are two major camps regarding heal-ing and its relationship to the atonement. On one side are those who see healing as a special gift of grace given only to some. Although they agree that healing was included in the plan of redemption, these folks do not view sickness as a curse that was removed through the atonement of Jesus Christ. On the other side is the camp that firmly believes healing to be a part of man's redemption in Christ, and that it therefore be-longs to every believer.

Healing as a Special Grace

The most prevalent view in the body of Christ concerning healing is that it is a gift of special grace. This theory supposes that God still heals as long as it is in His will to do so. If God does not wish to heal a particular individual, then no amount of faith will bring healing. The afflicted must be resigned to consider the sickness as the will of God.

With this view, there is no steadfast faith for healing. It is almost impossible to exercise persistent faith because, according to this perspective, if healing does not manifest, the assumption is that God does not wish to heal you—at least, not now. How should a person pray for healing? Well, since faith is not very important, people who hold to this view depend more on God's sovereignty than on personal faith. They generally pray something like this: "Lord, if it is Your will, please heal me."

A person can have sure faith only if he holds to the view that healing is in God's redemptive plan.

Of course, in the Bible, the emphasis is not on God's sovereignty but on faith. Jesus repeatedly said to the sick, *"Your faith has healed you"* (Matthew 9:22; Mark 10:52; Luke 8:48, 18:42). Never once did He say, "God's sovereignty has healed you."

There is no solid faith with the viewpoint of special grace. A person can have sure faith only if he holds to the view that healing is in God's redemptive plan. He can pray with faith, "Father, in the name of Jesus, according to Your Word, Jesus took my infirmities and carried my diseases, and by His stripes, I am healed. I stand on Your Word that I am healed. Thank You for healing me now, in Jesus' name."

Do you see how your view determines your level of faith when you pray for healing? Remember what Jesus said about prayer:

Therefore I tell you, whatever you ask for in prayer, believe that you have received it, and it will be yours. (Mark 11:24)

Sin Brought Sickness

Let's start at the beginning. Where did sickness come from in the first place? Did God create this world filled with diseases? Since sickness is so universal, many people attribute the origin of illness to God. The Bible, however, provides a different reason for the existence of sickness on the earth.

According to Scripture, when the world was made, *"God saw all that he had made, and it was very good"* (Genesis 1:31).

God did not originally create a world filled with anything bad. Everything was good. The Bible also teaches that something awful took place when Adam sinned against God. The apostle Paul wrote that *"sin entered the world through one man, and death through sin, and in this way death came to all men, because all sinned"* (Romans 5:12).

The result of sin was death. What is sickness? Sickness is an agent of death. It desires to kill and destroy. Without sickness, death would be postponed for most people. Sin brought death, and sickness is the offspring of its parent—death.

Sickness exists because sin exists.

In other words, sickness entered the world through sin. Without sin, there would be no sickness. To put it another way, sickness exists because sin exists.

During Jesus' ministry, His disciples once asked Him about the origin of sickness:

> *His disciples asked* [Jesus], *"Rabbi, who sinned, this man or his parents, that he was born blind?" "Neither this man nor his parents sinned," said Jesus, "but this happened so that the work of God might be displayed in his life."* (John 9:2–3)

You might read this and think that Jesus was contradicting what I just stated. But look at this Scripture carefully. The disciples knew sickness was caused by sin; they just wanted to know whose sin was at fault in causing the boy to be born blind. They determined that either the boy had sinned in the womb or his parents had sinned.

Jesus answered, *"Neither this man nor his parents sinned."* Notice that Jesus did not say,

"No one sinned." He also did not say, "Sin doesn't cause disease." He said only that the three people mentioned—the man and his parents—were not responsible for the blind man's condition. Jesus could have used this as a golden opportunity to teach that sickness and sin are completely unrelated, but He did not. The reason: sickness certainly *can be* related to sin.

Another time, Jesus healed a man at a pool called Bethesda. Later, He met the man again and said, *"See, you are well again. Stop sinning or something worse may happen to you"* (John 5:14). Jesus accused the man's sin of causing his infirmity.

There is also the case of King David's adultery with Bathsheba. Their sinful union produced a child who was struck with an illness. Eventually, the prophet Nathan made David see the dreadful consequence of his sin.

> *Then David said to Nathan, "I have sinned against the LORD." Nathan replied, "The LORD has taken away your sin. You are not going to die. But because by doing this you have made the enemies of the LORD show utter contempt, the son born to you will die."*
> (2 Samuel 12:13–14)

As we all know now, pollution and second-hand cigarette smoke can cause diseases. It's not hard to imagine an innocent child developing emphysema or asthma because of inhaling her parents' cigarette smoke, is it? In this way, even today, one person's sickness can be caused by another person's sin.

Through the atonement, the effects of sin can be removed from the repentant sinner.

It may be original sin, personal sin, or another person's sin, but sin brings with it sickness and disease.

In Christianity, the cure for sin is found in the atonement. This refers to Jesus Christ's suffering for the sins of mankind by His death on the cross and His to resurrection from the dead. Through the atonement, the effects of sin can be removed from the repentant sinner. It is the payment due that corrects, or satisfies, the relationship between God and man that was broken through sin.

How is healing connected to the atonement? Well, since sin causes disease, the cure for sickness must also be the atonement—the removal of the effects of sin. If a person's sickness comes on the wings of sin, the true remedy can be found in the redemption that comes from the atoning death and resurrection of Jesus Christ.

In many cases, it is this redemption—not doctors, medicine, or diet—that is the remedy for sickness. In such cases, the medical profession may help, but it will not heal.

Evangelical ministers often point to the cross for healing from emotional sickness and to doctors for healing from physical sickness. How inconsistent! Jesus is the cure for all diseases. Man's sickness is part of his curse, and who can remove the curse but God alone?

Old Testament Types of Healing

There are many examples in Scripture relating healing to the atonement.

The Passover

During the original Passover, God instructed all the households of Israel to take the blood of a lamb and apply it to the doorframes of their houses. God said that, as a result of seeing the blood, *"No destructive plague will touch you when I strike Egypt"* (Exodus 12:13). Because of the blood of the Passover lamb, no plague was permitted to touch the Israelites, and they were preserved in health. For Christians, of course, the Passover is a prophecy of the atonement of Christ. *"Christ, our Passover lamb, has been sacrificed"* (1 Corinthians 5:7).

Notice that the atonement kept the nation of Israel healthy. *"He brought them forth also with silver and gold: and there was not one feeble person among their tribes"* (Psalm 105:37 KJV). The word *"feeble"* means "weak." No one was weak physically when he came out of Egypt. Forget what you saw in the movie *The Ten Commandments*. No one was on crutches; no one was blind; no one died on the way. The blood of the lamb healed everyone!

If the blood of lambs could heal an entire nation, don't you think that the blood of the Lamb of God can heal everyone in the body of Christ? Of course it can!

Atonement Stops the Plague

There is another great example of the atonement bringing healing in the book of Numbers. As the Israelites wandered the desert on their way to the Promised Land, they grumbled against Moses and Aaron. As a result, a plague hit Israel. What was God's answer for this plague? Not simply prayer for mercy, but prayer for atonement, as well.

> *Then Moses said to Aaron, "Take your censer and put incense in it, along with fire from the altar, and hurry to the assembly to make atonement for them. Wrath has come out from the LORD; the plague has started." So Aaron did as Moses said, and ran into the midst of the assembly. The plague had already started among the people, but Aaron offered the incense and made atonement for them. He stood between the living and the dead, and the plague stopped.*
>
> (Numbers 16:46–48)

The plague stopped when an act of atonement was made. If healing is not connected to the atonement, why did the atonement protect the people? It is clear that the atonement was the cure for the plague.

A Bronze Snake

Another wonderful example of the atonement as it relates to healing is found in Numbers 21. Once again, the Israelites brought judgment on themselves, and they were bitten by poisonous snakes.

> *The reality of Christ's atonement can heal us from any diseases Satan tries to put on us.*

Snakes in Scripture speak of Satan. Satan himself had bitten the Israelites and caused them to suffer extreme nausea and pain. He's still doing this today. God's cure for His people was simple: *"So Moses made a bronze snake and put it up on a pole. Then when anyone was bitten by a snake and looked at the bronze snake, he lived"* (Numbers 21:9).

Jesus said of His own crucifixion: *"Just as Moses lifted up the snake in the desert, so the Son of Man must be lifted up"* (John 3:14). The bronze snake foreshadows the atonement of Christ. If the atonement could heal Israel from the venom of the snakes, surely the reality of Christ's atonement can heal us from any diseases Satan tries to put on us.

A Leper's Healing

According to Jewish law, if a leper was healed of his disease, the priest was to make atonement for him. Look at the following Scripture:

> The LORD said to Moses, "These are the regulations for the diseased person at the time of his ceremonial cleansing, when he is brought to the priest: The priest is to go outside the camp and examine him. If the person has been healed of his infectious skin disease, the priest shall order that two live clean birds and some cedar wood, scarlet yarn and hyssop be brought for the one to be cleansed....Then the priest is to sacrifice the sin offering and make atonement for the one to be cleansed from his uncleanness. After that, the priest shall slaughter the burnt offering and offer it on the altar, together with the grain offering, and make atonement for him, and he will be clean."
> (Leviticus 14:1–4, 19–20)

Here is my question: Why was atonement made for the leper's healing if there is no healing available in the atonement of Christ?

Clearly, healing is found in the atonement.

Many fundamentalists criticize Christian Scientists for believing that salvation can be attained without the atonement, yet fundamentalists make a similar blunder by separating healing from forgiveness, and by separating sickness from sin. This is wrong. Healing is attained through the atonement.

The Crucifixion of Christ

Now, let us direct our attention to the cross of Christ. First, look at a passage in Isaiah prophesying Jesus' crucifixion.

> *Surely he hath borne our griefs, and carried our sorrows: yet we did esteem him stricken, smitten of God, and afflicted. But he was wounded for our transgressions, he was bruised for our iniquities: the chastisement of our peace was upon him; and with his stripes we are healed.*
>
> (Isaiah 53:4–5 KJV)

The *Amplified Bible* translates verse 4 in Isaiah as follows: *"Surely He has borne our griefs (sicknesses, weaknesses, and distresses) and carried our sorrows and pains [of punishment]."*

Here, the word *"griefs"* is linked to disease. The Hebrew word for *"griefs"* is *choliy.* Often in Scripture, this word is translated as *"disease," "illness,"* or *"sickness."* (See, for example, Deuteronomy 7:15; 28:61; 1 Kings 17:17 KJV; 2 Kings 1:2 KJV; 8:8 KJV; 2 Chronicles 16:12; 21:15.) It is not referring to grief in the sense of an emotional sadness, but a sickness or physical disease.

As proof, the apostle Matthew used it to refer to sickness after Jesus physically healed Peter's mother-in-law from fever. Matthew referred to the passage in Isaiah as the scriptural basis of His healing ministry: *"This was to fulfill what was spoken through the prophet Isaiah: 'He took up our infirmities and carried our diseases'"* (Matthew 8:17). Clearly, Matthew interpreted Isaiah's passage about the atonement of the Messiah to cover physical healing as well as spiritual healing.

A detractor of mine in El Paso was constantly criticizing me publicly on the radio. Finally, he asked if he could meet with me, and I reluctantly consented. After arriving, he wanted to discuss divine healing. He believed that God was able to heal but denied that health was included in the atonement.

First, I led him to Isaiah 53, but he argued that Jesus bore only our *spiritual* diseases, which he interpreted to mean sin. Then, I showed him that Matthew disagreed with him about the meaning of Isaiah because he quoted the verse in reference to Jesus' physical healing ministry.

Then, he changed his tactic by claiming that Isaiah 53:4 covered only Jesus' temporary healing ministry on the earth, and he maintained that it was not about the atonement.

I looked at him and said, "If you are right, then we are all going to hell."

He was shocked and said, "What do you mean?"

"It's simple," I said. "You are saying that the infirmities and diseases Jesus *'hath borne...and carried'* were only the infirmities of people during Jesus' earthly ministry. If that is so, then, according to your argument, He does not carry *our* sicknesses and diseases, but only *theirs*. Right?"

"Uh," he said with a nod, "I guess so."

"Well then, we are still in our sins, because the next verse of Isaiah says, *'But he was pierced for **our** transgressions, he was crushed for **our** iniquities'* (Isaiah 53:5, emphasis added). If the sicknesses He took up and the diseases He carried were not really *ours*, then the transgressions and iniquities He carried were not *ours*, either."

> *The cross is eternal. It is the only basis for forgiveness and healing.*

He thought for a moment. "You make a good point, but why does Matthew quote the atonement passage in reference to the healing ministry of Christ that precedes the cross?"

"My brother, it is quite simple. Christ is the Lamb of God that was *'slain from the foundation of the world'* (Revelation 13:8 KJV). The cross is eternal. It is the only basis for forgiveness and healing—for those who lived before the cross and for those who live after the cross. It is eternal redemption. Not only did Jesus heal based on the eternal redemption of the cross, but He also forgave sinners based on the cross."

Physical Disease

As I preached this message in my church, a young man named Joel came forward for prayer. He had broken his leg in a skateboarding accident, and the doctors felt the break was so severe that it was likely he would need extensive surgery. As he heard me preach, he developed the opinion that physical healing was his. As he stood up for prayer, I called out various healings taking place. Joel was one of those healed. Without the aid of a single crutch, he ran up to the platform to testify to his total healing. His wife, who had been sitting next to him, wept with joy.

Many argue that physical healing is not provided for in the atonement, but Joel believed differently, and he received physical healing.

By His Stripes

The most important phrase that has been used in connection with healing is this: *"With his stripes we are healed"* (Isaiah 53:5 KJV). Peter referenced this verse in his own epistle: *"By whose stripes ye were healed"* (1 Peter 2:24 KJV).

The stripes are a clear reference to the whipping Jesus received from the soldier ordered to flog Him. It was customary to use a whip with little pieces of bone or stone tied on at the end. The soldier would strap a man to a pole and then whip him forty times. In Scripture, forty represents the number of completion. Moses and Jesus both fasted for forty days. Noah's flood lasted for forty days.

Jesus suffered the completed number of stripes to fully heal you. Nothing is left to be done for your complete healing.

It was often the custom, however, for soldiers to leave out one strike. The apostle Paul alluded to this practice: *"Five times I received from the Jews the forty lashes minus one"* (2 Corinthians 11:24). That extra lash was left out in case the person was accidentally whipped one time too many. Basically, a lash was left off in case they had miscounted.

People often ask, "If God keeps healing us of every disease, how will we ever die?" I find it humorous that people are worried about this. Certainly, the human race has had no difficulty dying. The truth is, nearly every saint—whether strong or weak in faith for healing—will succumb to one last illness that will take him to glory. Lazarus was miraculously raised from the dead, but even he eventually succumbed to the inevitability of death.

I believe in the complete healing of all my diseases, but I also know there will be a time for me to leave this earth after I have completed my work here. At the end of my life, someone may say, "His heart gave out," and it will be called a heart attack. Or he may say, "He stopped breathing," and it will be labeled lung disease. It does not matter to me. I fully expect the Lord to heal me of all my diseases, but I am not foolish enough to think that I will not die. It will happen to me and to everyone who believes in Christ. We will go home to be with the Lord. Amen!

My point is that God still laid every disease on the back of Jesus as He was whipped. If your diseases were laid on Him, why try to carry them yourself? Believe that by His stripes you are healed. Confess out loud that you are healed by His stripes.

> *Physical healing is a great benefit of the cross, but it is only one part of complete healing.*

Physical healing is a great benefit of the cross, but it is only one part of complete healing. In the next section, we are going to look at complete wholeness and not merely physical wholeness. Healing is more than being free from organic, bodily disease. It is being free in your mind and emotions, as well.

Part II

Mental Diseases

Chapter Six

Healing for the Whole Man

Some time later, Jesus went up to Jerusalem for a feast of the Jews. Now there is in Jerusalem near the Sheep Gate a pool, which in Aramaic is called Bethesda and which is surrounded by five covered colonnades. Here a great number of disabled people used to lie—the blind, the lame, the paralyzed. One who was there had been an invalid for thirty-eight years. When Jesus saw him lying there and learned that he had been in this condition for a long time, he asked him, "Do you want to get well?" "Sir," the invalid replied, "I have no one to help me into the pool when the water is stirred. While I am trying to get in, someone else goes down ahead of me." Then Jesus said to him, "Get up! Pick up your mat and walk." At once the man was cured; he picked up his mat and walked. The day *on which this took place was a Sabbath.... Later Jesus found him at the temple and said to him, "See, you are well again. Stop sinning or something worse may happen to you."* (John 5:1–9, 14)

Let's take a look at Jesus' commentary on this man's healing:

Jesus said to them, "I did one miracle, and you are all astonished. Yet, because Moses gave you circumcision (though actually it did not come from Moses, but from the patriarchs), you circumcise a child on the Sabbath. Now if a child can be circumcised on the Sabbath so that the law of Moses may not be broken, why are you angry with me for healing the whole man on the Sabbath?" (John 7:21–23)

The phrase that sticks out to me is *"why are you angry with me for healing the whole man...?"* Jesus healed not just *part* of the man but the *whole* man, the total man, the complete man.

There was more wrong with this man than what was initially evident. At first glance, it seems that all he needed was physical healing. But a closer examination reveals far more. Jesus said, *"Stop sinning or something worse may happen to you"* (John 5:14). Apparently, this man had a sin problem as well as a health problem. Most people who attend miracle crusades or healing services are looking for physical healing. Sometimes, however, they need more than a physical cure; they also need spiritual healing. In other words, they need to be healed from sin.

But that's not all this man was dealing with. He also had an attitude problem. Jesus asked him if he wanted to be healed, and the man complained, *"I have no one to help me"* (verse 7). He felt sorry for himself and was making excuses. Some people need healing in their attitudes. He continued his complaint in the same verse: *"While I am trying to get in, someone else goes down ahead of me."*

For some people, it is always someone else's fault, never their own. Do you know people like that? Maybe you recognize a bad attitude in your own life. Jesus has come to heal your attitude as well as your body and your spirit.

> *Jesus has come to heal the whole man, not just part of man.*

The point of this story is simple: Jesus has come to heal the *whole* man, not just *part* of man. He has come to heal you completely, not partially. This is what deliverance healing can accomplish. The three areas that need healing are our spirits, souls, and bodies.

What Is Man?

How do we know that man is composed of spirit, soul, and body? God tells us so. God's Word is the scalpel that dissects mankind for us so that we can know our makeup. Every student in medical school has to dissect a cadaver in order to learn about the human body, which he will be healing. In order for medical students to be able to heal the body, they must know what it consists of.

Since Jesus came to heal the whole man, it is important to understand the totality of man. There is more to us than meets the eye. Even the psalmist wondered, *"What is man…?"* (Psalm 8:4).

This ancient question must be answered. The only One who truly knows man is God. Because He is the Creator, He knows the complexity of His creation.

If I drive a Toyota, I will not take it to a Ford dealership to be serviced. I will take it to its manufacturer. When you are sick, you also need to go to the manufacturer. Your Manufacturer is God. As much as doctors can help, they really do not have a full understanding of the complexity of mankind's makeup.

In the last century, we saw the birth of a new science called *psychiatry*. It was born from the medical world's realization that our minds affect our health. Dealing with an illness of the mind is not as simple as cutting out a tumor or medicating a disease. The more science studies the human species, the more it realizes how complex we really are.

Who is man? The answer must come from God. Only He made us, and only He can tell us who we are. And He tells us through His Word—the Bible.

Spirit, Soul, and Body

May God himself, the God of peace, sanctify you through and through. May your whole spirit, soul and body be kept blameless at the coming of our Lord Jesus Christ.

(1 Thessalonians 5:23)

We need blessing and healing through and through. In this passage, the apostle Paul exclaimed, *"May your whole spirit, soul and body...."* Not just part of you, but all of you. Jesus does not only want you healed, He also wants you whole. He wants you complete, not lacking anything! Paul mentions three parts to us: spirit, soul, and body.

> *Jesus does not only want you healed, He also wants you whole. He wants you complete, not lacking anything!*

It was the custom of the writers in Paul's day to list things in order of importance. In this instance, it is clear that the spirit is the most important part of the whole man. It is our God-side. Our spirits desire to fellowship with God. Our spirits refuse to allow us to disbelieve in God's existence. As hard as atheists try, they can't shake off their unconscious awareness of God's existence.

Paul also mentioned the soul and the body. There you have all three parts of man mentioned in the New Testament. I believe Paul received this revelation about man's three-part nature through the Old Testament, primarily from the two creation accounts.

Dust and Breath

The first creation account (Genesis 1) emphasizes the nobility of man. The second creation account (Genesis 2) reveals the humility of man.

The First Creation Account

Then God said, "Let us make man in our image, in our likeness, and let them rule over the fish of the sea and the birds of the air, over the livestock, over all the earth, and over all the creatures that move along the ground." So God created man in his own image, in the image of God he created him; male and female he created them.

(Genesis 1:26–27)

The first account reveals three important things about man:

1. He is made in God's image.

2. He has dominion over the animals.

3. He enjoys a different food source from the animals.

I am awestruck when I read this! We are made in God's image. God Himself was the pattern for man. Then, He reminds us that we should rule the animals:

> *God blessed them and said to them, "Be fruitful and increase in number; fill the earth and subdue it. Rule over the fish of the sea and the birds of the air and over every living creature that moves on the ground."* (Genesis 1:28)

According to God, you are in charge of creation, which also means you must take care of creation. We are the only species that cares about preserving all other species.

We are made in God's image. God Himself was the pattern for man.

To highlight man's supremacy and nobility over the rest of creation, God gave mankind a different food source.

> *Then God said, "I give you every seed-bearing plant on the face of the whole earth and every tree that has fruit with seed in it. They will be yours for food. And to all the beasts of the earth and all the birds of the air and all the creatures that move on the ground—everything that has the breath of*

life in it—I give every green plant for food."
And it was so.   (Genesis 1:29–30)

How does this relate to man's supremacy? Animals cannot appreciate the law of sowing and reaping. God reminds man that he should. Even Jesus commented, *"Look at the birds of the air; they do not sow or reap or store away in barns, and yet your heavenly Father feeds them. Are you not much more valuable than they?"* (Matthew 6:26). We are much more valuable than animals, because, for one thing, we have an understanding of seedtime and harvest.

The Second Creation Account

And the LORD God formed man of the dust of the ground, and breathed into his nostrils the breath of life; and man became a living soul.   (Genesis 2:7 KJV)

The second creation account reveals some additional interesting facts about man:

1. Man was formed from dust.

2. Man has a spirit that comes from God.

3. Man is an eternal soul.

Let's look at the first fact. With all the noble things God said about man, there is the somewhat humiliating fact that we are formed from dirt. The passage says that *"God formed man of the dust of the ground."* It does not seem that we are that much different from the animals. In fact, scientists have discovered that the difference between a gorilla and a human is only that of one chromosome. Our genes are only fractions different from rodents'.

How can this be? Animals come from the same source as man.

Now the Lord *God had formed out of the ground all the beasts of the field and all the birds of the air. He brought them to the man to see what he would name them; and whatever the man called each living creature, that was its name.* (Genesis 2:19)

God formed the animals from the ground— the same source that man was formed from. Perhaps this is why medical scientists can experiment on rats to find cures for people.

This passage, however, also shows man's nobility. He is noble in that he names the animals. The giver of a name denotes authority, much as a parent names a child or an entrepreneur names a company. Man is in charge of the animals, yet the passage also reveals that man comes from the dust of the ground. Looking closely at Genesis 2:7 (KJV), we again see three important aspects of man's origin:

1. Man's body was formed from the dust of the ground. Physically, we are like animals.

2. God breathed into man the breath of life. Breath speaks of spirit.

In fact, the Hebrew and Greek words for *spirit* can also be translated as "breath" or "wind." Since Jesus called God a spirit (see John 4:24), we see that God took something of Himself and put it into man. In simple language, God *"breathed into his nostrils the breath of life"* (Genesis 2:7 KJV). God took His own substance—His own essence—and put it into man. In this way, man has a spirit made in the likeness of God.

But notice carefully that God breathed into man's *nostrils* the breath of life. He did not breathe into his mouth. God did not do mouth-to-mouth resuscitation. If you can imagine the picture, God is breathing into man's nostrils, which puts God on a higher level than man. God reminds man that no matter how close he is to being like God, he still is lower than God. In fact, the psalmist exclaimed, *"For thou hast made him but little lower than God, and crownest him with glory and honor"* (Psalm 8:5 ASV). Man is crowned with glory and honor, yet he still remains a *"little lower than God."*

3. The result of the union of spirit and body was the soul. *"Man became a living soul"* (Genesis 2:7 KJV).

Man did not receive a soul. A soul was not created for him. No! He *became* a soul. A soul is what we are! We are not bodies or spirits. We are souls who have bodies and spirits. But the thing that makes us human is our soul. It is what separates us from being like animals, or even from being like God.

In conclusion, our bodies relate to animals, our spirits relate to God, and our souls relate to the human race. Or, to put it another way, our bodies make us like animals, our spirits make us like God, and our souls make us like other humans.

Chapter Seven

What Is the Soul?

Man became a living soul. —Genesis 2:7 KJV

Those words describe what we became. We would love to be living spirits. It seems like a great thing to be able to be like God. It is man's desire to be like He is. But this desire, however noble it may seem, became the cause of man's greatest failure. The serpent crept up to Eve and told her to go ahead and eat the forbidden fruit, *"for God knows that when you eat of it your eyes will be opened, and you will be like God, knowing good and evil"* (Genesis 3:5).

Perhaps Adam and Eve were tired of being human. This was their chance to become divine. No longer would they remain a little lower than God; they would be equal to Him. How wrong they were!

But this is the same dilemma that mankind faces today. Are we willing to allow the Creator to rule our souls, or do we want our souls to rule our lives? The last line of *Invictus*, the well-known poem by Victorian poet William Ernest Henley, states, "...I am the captain of my soul." Once you become the captain of your soul, you will soon discover how unqualified a guide you really are.

The Mind

> *You cannot have a soul without a spirit.*

Since we are living souls, it would do us good to define what is meant by the soul. The Hebrew word for *soul* is *nephesh*, meaning "that which breathes." This is related to the breath of God. God is spirit. He breathed and man inhaled, and so was born the soul. This, however, does not tell us much about the soul. It shows only how closely the soul is related to the spirit. You cannot have a soul without a spirit.

The New Testament, written in Greek, helps us to better define the soul. The Greek word it uses for *soul* is *psuche*. This means "breath," but it also carries the meaning of the rational and immortal side to us. In other words, soul refers to the mind. This is where the word *psyche* comes from.

Proverbs 23:7 says, *"As [a man] thinketh in his heart, so is he"* (KJV). You are the sum total of your thoughts. Let me illustrate this.

Suppose your arm was amputated, and my arm was attached in its place. Would you become me? Not at all. You would continue to be yourself with my arm. Suppose you lost both your arms, and they were replaced with my arms. Would you no longer be yourself? Of course not. The same would be true if your legs, eyes, or any other part of your body were lost and replaced with similar parts from somebody else. You would still remain you. No matter how many body parts you received as replacements, those parts would not change your personality.

But suppose you kept all your other parts, yet my brain replaced yours. You would look and sound the same, yet you would undergo a fundamental change of personality. If my mind was put into your body, then my personality would also shift into your body. Although you would look like you, you would actually be me! Why? Because your mind is who you are. You are your soul. *"Man became a living soul"* (Genesis 2:7 KJV). That is who you are. You are a soul. You are a mind. The real you is found in your thoughts!

The Butterfly

The real change God wants to make in us must occur in our minds. In ancient Greek, the word *psuche* is also the word for "butterfly." A caterpillar undergoes metamorphosis and becomes a butterfly. Paul used this analogy to speak of being *"transformed by the renewing of your mind"* (Romans 12:2). The word *"transformed"* in Greek is the word *metamorphoo*, which, as you see, is where we get our word *metamorphose*. There may be no greater transformation in nature than that of a caterpillar into a butterfly. If God had not breathed into man, man would be no different from the animals. But man was transformed into a soul.

> **The mind is our greatest asset, but it is also the source of our greatest problems.**

Mankind's predominant feature is his mind. Giraffes are known for their necks, whales for their size, and cheetahs for their speed, but humans are known for their minds. This is what Genesis 2 was saying: man became a living soul, a living mind.

So, the seat of the soul is the mind, which comprises emotions, intellect, and reasoning ability. The mind is our greatest asset, but it is also the source of our greatest problems.

Rest for Your Souls

Look around you, and you will see a lot of sick people. They are sick not only in their bodies but also in their souls. Why are they sick? They are sick because they are restless. They do not want to allow Christ to guide their souls. Jesus wants to rescue us from our burdens.

Come to me, all you who are weary and burdened, and I will give you rest. Take my yoke upon you and learn from me, for I am gentle and humble in heart, and you will find rest for your souls. For my yoke is easy and my burden is light.

(Matthew 11:28–30)

The word *disease* is based on two words: *dis*, meaning "not," and *ease*, meaning "rest." *Disease* literally means "not at ease" or "not at rest." That is the *real* disease. Our society is not at rest but in turmoil. Americans pride themselves on being strong and hardworking. Yet Americans—who make up only 6 percent of the world's population—consume 90 percent of the world's tranquilizers. Of the ten leading causes of disability worldwide in 2000, five were psychiatric conditions: depression, alcohol addiction, bipolar disorder, schizophrenia, and obsessive compulsive disorder.[2] An estimated 26 percent (more than 1 in 4) of American adults have a mental disorder.[3] According to the International Society of Psychiatric-Mental Health Nurses, psychiatric conditions account for almost 11 percent of the disease burden worldwide.[4]

Daytime talk shows often highlight the truth of our troubled society: people throwing chairs, screaming obscenities, fighting, pulling hair,

---

[2] G. H. Brundtland, "Mental Health in the 21st Century," *Bulletin of the World Health Organization* 78, no. 4 (2000): 411.

[3] R. C. Kessler, and others, "Prevalence, Severity, and Comorbidity of Twelve-month DSM-IV Disorders in the National Comorbidity Survey Replication (NCS-R)," *Archives of General Psychiatry* 62, no. 6 (June 2005): 617–27.

[4] www.ispn-psych.org/docs/4-00Global-Burden.pdf.

and much worse. And the ratings go up because a viewing public wants to see more. Perhaps they feel better if they can see people who are more disturbed than they are. Is this what we have become?

Isn't it clear that mankind is not healthy? An unknown author penned a poem describing the problem. It could be our national anthem:

> We mutter and sputter;
> We fume and we spurt;
> We mumble and grumble;
> Our feelings get hurt.
> We can't understand things.
> Our vision grows dim,
> When all that we need is
> A moment with Him!

More than the Mind

The soul is not the brain. The brain is simply the organ that houses our thoughts in this life. Beyond this life, however, our thoughts continue, because, in reality, the soul is that invisible, immortal part of you that makes up your personality and affects your mind and emotions. Look at what Jesus said about the soul: *"Do not be afraid of those who kill the body but cannot kill the soul"* (Matthew 10:28).

The soul cannot die. The brain may die, but our souls will continue beyond the grave.

What good is it for a man to gain the whole world, yet forfeit his soul?　　(Mark 8:36)

What good is it for a man to gain the whole world, and yet lose or forfeit his very self?
　　　　　　　　　　　　　(Luke 9:25)

From these two parallel passages, we can easily conclude that the *"soul"* is the *"very self."* Your soul, therefore, is more than your mind; it is the real self that determines what you think. Part of the reason for the restlessness you feel is your wrong thoughts.

Demons Come to Destroy the Soul

A demon does not come simply to make your body sick. Why should the demon bother with something as insignificant as the body when the soul is far more enticing? Of course, demons attack the body, too, but the soul is worth far more. When people come to my crusades for healing, they often limit that healing to their bodies, but they quickly learn that they need healing for their souls, as well.

> *Scripture is quick to point out that Satan and his demons are eager to attack the mind.*

Scripture is quick to point out that Satan and his demons are eager to attack the mind.

But I am afraid that just as Eve was deceived by the serpent's cunning, your minds may somehow be led astray from

113

your sincere and pure devotion to Christ.

(2 Corinthians 11:3)

It is clear here that Satan will try to deceive you by leading *"your minds"* astray. If Satan has your mind, he has you. Therefore, demons work primarily on the mind.

If Satan has your mind, he has you. Therefore, demons work primarily on the mind.

Consider the apostle Paul's statement about spiritual warfare:

For though we live in the world, we do not wage war as the world does. The weapons we fight with are not the weapons of the world. On the contrary, they have divine power to demolish strongholds. We demolish arguments and every pretension that sets itself up against the knowledge of God, and we take captive every thought to make it obedient to Christ.

(2 Corinthians 10:3–5)

"Arguments and every pretension" are part of the mind. Spiritual warfare is, therefore, a war in the mind.

Emotions

Emotions are the easiest part of the soul for Satan and his demons to attack. Usually, when someone is being attacked by demons, his emotions are the first thing to buckle under the strain. In such cases, people will often suffer nervous breakdowns or, at the very least, severe panic attacks.

If you experience panic attacks, you may feel dizzy or nauseated. More than just feeling sick, you may have the sense that reality is slipping away. You may feel that you're starting to lose your sanity, or even that you are going to die. Your heart may feel like it is beating out of your chest. You can't catch your breath. You break out in a cold sweat. You want to escape.

These attacks can cripple your activity. Whenever you anticipate anxiety, you will avoid any situations in which you have had previous attacks. Thus, you may refuse to go out alone, and you may begin to develop any number of terrifying phobias. Is this your experience? Such attacks are from Satan. He is putting thoughts into your mind. Thankfully, you can overcome him through the Word of God.

My stepfather, Red, once suffered from debilitating panic attacks. He felt that he was going crazy. He wanted freedom but did not have the answer. Then, one Sunday morning, I was teaching on the power of the spoken Word of God. I explained that Jesus used only one weapon against Satan—He spoke the written Scriptures out loud. And whenever He did, Satan left. I then gave my church a list of several Scriptures to speak out loud every day of their lives.

Red began to think, *This is my answer. I am going to speak the Word of God!* When the next panic attack came, he opened his mouth and began to speak the Word of God. Later, he described the experience: "I could feel the black cloud over me suddenly vanish when I began to confess the Word of God." Today, Red is zealous in telling his story to anyone suffering from panic attacks. The Word works!

Maybe you don't have anxiety attacks, but, nevertheless, you are not at rest. How can you tell when you are not at rest? The psalmist described a soul that is not at rest with these words: *"I said, 'Oh, that I had the wings of a dove! I would fly away and be at rest'"* (Psalm 55:6).

Emotions are a part of the soul. *Emotion* comes from the Latin word *emovere*. The prefix *e-* (or *ex-*) means "out," and *movere* means "move." Thus, it means "to move away." When you feel like moving away, you are not at rest. Do you feel like you want to escape? Do you feel the urge to leave your city, your job, or, worse, your family? What is happening? Your soul is being attacked by demons.

If your soul is being attacked by demons, take courage and know that by the power of God and His Word, you can get rid of them and be free.

Chapter Eight

The Spirit of Fear

For God hath not given us the spirit of fear; but of power, and of love, and of a sound mind. —2 Timothy 1:7 KJV

You do not have to wonder about the source of fear. This Scripture is blunt. Fear is a *"spirit."* Fear is a demon.

For you did not receive a spirit that makes you a slave again to fear. (Romans 8:15)

This Scripture refers to a spirit that *"makes you a slave."* Sure, fear can stir and affect your emotions, but there is more to fear than emotional distress. Make no mistake; fear is not merely an emotion; it is also a spiritual force.

I am sometimes asked by reporters how I can tell whether a person's emotional problems are demonic or simply psychological. The Bible teaches that the roots of psychological problems are demonic, but the fruit may be in the form of emotional symptoms. You may see fruit on the tree, but the life force of the fruit is in the roots hidden underground. You can't see the roots, but they are there.

In other words, the fruit can be seen through symptoms—fear, depression, anxieties—but the root is the invisible operation of demons. A psychologist can rightly diagnose someone as having a certain phobia (the fruit), but the diagnosis falls short of explaining the source (the root) of the phobia.

> **Fear is produced by demons speaking words into your mind.**

People are usually relieved to discover the sources of their phobias. It is much easier to deal with the specific spirits producing the fear than to try to deal with some abstract cause. Fear is produced by demons speaking words into your mind. As we saw in the previous chapter, you must *"take captive every thought to make it obedient to Christ"* (2 Corinthians 10:5). Those thoughts may try to run wild, but you must imprison and confine them to the judgment of God.

The Good Kind of Fear

Granted, there are some fears that are normal and not demonic. In fact, some fears are good. The Bible tells us, *"The fear of the LORD is the beginning of knowledge"* (Proverbs 1:7). Thus, not every fear is awful or harmful.

For example, another word for *fear* is *caution*. *Eulabeia* is the Greek word for "caution, circumspection, discretion, avoidance." It is the mechanism that helps us deal with danger and keeps us from acting like foolish daredevils.

This kind of fear is short-lived. We face it during moments of crisis. For example, my son Justin once developed a swollen eye. Obviously, we were concerned about him. That concern turned into positive action on our part. We took him to the doctor and discovered that he had a rare infection that, if left untreated, could have resulted in the loss of his eye. The doctor prescribed medicine for him and told us to keep an eye on him (pun intended). The doctor told us that if the swelling did not go down within two days, we should rush him to the hospital. After twenty-four hours, I noticed no improvement. I felt led by the Lord to look at the expiration date on the medicine bottle, and I found that it expired that day. So, I made the pharmacy exchange the medicine. Within hours the swelling went down.

The concerned kind of fear is actually good and helpful. It serves to protect us from danger and harm. Some people actually prefer to call it concern instead of fear. Regardless of what you name it, you must not confuse this with negative, demonic fear.

I remember hearing the story of a woman who lifted a car off the ground to save her child. She had been involved in a serious accident, and the car had flipped on its side and on top of her child, who was caught underneath. Without thinking, the woman rushed out of the car, lifted it up, and pulled her child to safety. What gave her that strength? It was the fear that her child would die.

This type of fear gives us a boost of adrenaline for our own protection, as well as the protection of others. We call upon it often to overcome obstacles and to perform to the best of our abilities. I remember watching the best quarterback ever to play pro football, Joe Montana, as he scrambled away from a horde of large and angry defensive pass rushers. He thrived on performing in clutch situations and in the face of danger. It always seemed that the more hopeless the situation was, the better he played. This is an example of a good kind of fear, which can also be called caution, or vigilance.

"Fear Hath Torment"

Sometimes, however, fear will not end. For example, as a result of her traumatic experience, the mother who rescued her child in the previous story might become afraid to drive, or she might become overprotective. When such a reaction is the case, we are no longer dealing with healthy fear but unhealthy fear. Unhealthy fear does not stop. It is the kind of fear John talked about when he wrote, *"Fear hath torment"* (1 John 4:18 KJV).

The Greek word for *"fear"* here is *phobos*. It gives us our word *phobia*. This type of fear no longer enables you to overcome or perform better but instead haunts and torments you. It is demonic.

This fear hinders the believer from enjoying life and freezes him or her from doing the will of God. It may be the fear of flying. You may be called to serve in the mission fields overseas, but the fear of flying grips you and prevents you from going. You want to visit relatives out of town, but it suddenly seems too dangerous to travel, so you stay home instead. This is illogical. You are overcome by fear, and it has made you irrational. You grow afraid of crowds, and it keeps you from going to church.

There are all kinds of phobias that hinder people from enjoying the abundant life that Jesus came to give them.

There are all kinds of phobias that hinder people from enjoying the abundant life that Jesus came to give them. (See John 10:10.) If fear has that effect in your life, it is probably demonic, in which case you need to overcome it.

Delivered from All Your Fears

I know a man who was afraid to hold hands in prayer. He felt that his hands would curse other people. He knew it was irrational, but it took the power of God to deliver him. Today, he is one of the greatest prayer warriors I know.

The psalmist experienced deliverance from fears: *"I sought the LORD, and he answered me; he delivered me from all my fears"* (Psalm 34:4).

The answer for fear is deliverance. *"He delivered me from all my fears."* Deliverance is instant. People rarely overcome fear gradually. When they try to do so, they usually find themselves worse off than before. God will deliver you from the demonic spirits that have put you in bondage to fear.

I remember when my youngest son, Caleb, was deathly afraid of fireworks. He would bury his head in his lap, close his ears, and try to shut out the noise. One year, on the Fourth of July, we were awaiting the fireworks display at the end of a baseball game. Caleb was about to follow his routine of burying his head when I stopped him. I said, "Caleb, you do not need to be afraid of fireworks. The Lord is about to deliver you from this fear."

He looked at me and said, "Really?"

I affirmed what I had said. Then, I took my hands and placed them on his head, and I drove out the spirit of fear. When I did, I said, "The spirit of fear has left you. You can now enjoy the fireworks."

He smiled, and as the fireworks began, he did not bat an eye. He looked up at the sky and enjoyed every blast afterward. He looked over at me, smiled, and said, "Dad, I'm not afraid anymore."

I believe in instant deliverance from fear. You don't have to wait to be delivered. You can experience it quickly and get over your fear.

Love, Power, and a Sound Mind

For God hath not given us the spirit of fear; but of power, and of love, and of a sound mind.　　　　(2 Timothy 1:7 KJV)

There are three forces that help us overcome our fears. Each force is mentioned in this Scripture: power, love, and a sound mind.

Fear Cannot Coexist with Power

Why do we fear? We fear because we feel powerless and helpless. We believe that we can't change something. As long as you have power to change some evil, then fear cannot take over.

> *As long as you have power to change some evil, then fear cannot take over.*

The Bible says, *"Resist the devil, and he will flee from you"* (James 4:7). We have the power to resist the devil, to make him flee from us. We can heal the sick. We can call on angels for our protection. We can overcome evil with good.

When you finally recognize that you have this kind of power available to you, fear cannot stay. Fear cannot coexist with power.

Love Drives Out Fear

The Bible also says that we have love, and that there is a direct correlation between love and fear.

There is no fear in love. But perfect love drives out fear, because fear has to do with punishment. The one who fears is not made perfect in love. (1 John 4:18)

Fear and love also cannot coexist. You have either love or fear; you cannot have both. This passage shows that the person who fears doubts God's love. When you know that God loves you, you know that He will help you, not harm you. We often fear because we think we deserve punishment. We think God is out to harm us. In reality, He is out to help us.

Many sermons have given the false impression that God causes trouble in the believer's life. Why do so many people believe that God would punish His children? They believe it because they doubt God's love for them.

I know that God loves me. I will not fear that God desires to punish me.

I can't speak for you, but I know that God loves me. I will

124

not fear that God desires to punish me. I know that the punishment for my sins has already been endured at the cross. God so loved me that He sent Jesus to take my place of punishment. My sins have already been punished. So, I rely on God's love for me—that He will reward and bless me.

Wired for Faith, Not Fear

The chief area that fear seems to attack is the mind. This is why Paul said that we must have a sound mind. God did not create your mind to handle fear. Your mind is not wired for fear. Stick a fork in an outlet, and you will discover that your body is not wired for electricity. Neither is your mind wired for fear.

I once read the story about an underclassman who took part in an initiation for a fraternity. The fraternity members blindfolded him and tied him to the railroad tracks. He did not know that the section of track he was tied to was disconnected from the main track. All he knew was that he heard the sound of an approaching train. As it got closer, he screamed for help. The fraternity brothers just laughed. Finally, after the train safely passed by, they went to untie the young man, only to discover that he had died from a heart attack.

Jesus spoke of *"men's hearts failing them for fear"* (Luke 21:26 KJV). You may not die as quickly as this freshman did, but you will experience another kind of death. You will begin to lose courage. Without courage, you will never be able to win your battles.

Demons Are Afraid

Isaiah prophesied what fear would do: *"Whoever flees at the sound of terror will fall into a pit"* (Isaiah 24:18).

The main weapon of terrorists is fear. The reason they use this weapon is that they are acquainted with it firsthand. Terrorists are afraid, themselves. They are afraid of losing their way of life. Those who attacked the United States on 9/11, for example, saw the country as bigger and stronger than they. They feared losing power. They feared that Christianity would wipe out their religion. So, they attacked our nation in order to make us fear them. But the truth is, they are more afraid of us than we are of them.

Fear breeds more fear. Demons are afraid, and they are giving you their emotions.

The same is true of demons. They are spirits of fear because they are fearful. Their presence brings fear. Fear breeds more fear. Demons are afraid, and they are giving you their emotions. *"You believe that there is one God. Good! Even the demons believe that—and shudder"* (James 2:19).

Demons quake with fear in God's presence. God lives in you, and demons should quake with fear when you know who you are in Christ. *"Be self-controlled and alert. Your enemy the devil prowls around like a roaring lion looking for someone to devour"* (1 Peter 5:8). Lions do not roar when they are ready to attack their prey. They roar only when they feel threatened. They roar to frighten away intruders. The devil roars to frighten you.

I have never met a lion, but I have met a Doberman pinscher. I was riding my bike when the dog ran into the street about thirty feet from me. My initial reaction was to pedal away as fast as I could, but I knew the dog would catch me. So, with my heart pounding in my chest, I jumped off my bike and ran directly toward him, screaming, "Ahhhhh!" The dog stopped, turned, and ran away from me! It turned out that he was more afraid of me than I was of him.

This is what James meant when he wrote, *"Resist the devil, and he will flee from you"* (James 4:7). The Greek word for *flee* means "to seek safety by flight." The devil is actually afraid of you, but he does not want you to know it. Whenever you feel fear, know for sure that the demons are even more afraid.

It's time that you purpose to live fear-free. Whenever you notice fear in your life, attack it by quoting the Word of God. Here is a confession based on the Word of God that you can use when you face fear:

> I fear not, for God has not given me the spirit of fear, but He has given me power, love, and a sound mind. I have a peaceful, quiet mind. I have the mind of Christ. I am not afraid, because God will provide for my children and my needs. I am not afraid, because I have more angels with me than there are demons with the enemy. I am not afraid, because I am worth more than sparrows. If God is for me, who can be against me? God is on my side!

Chapter Nine

The Demon of Depression

*D*epression is a modern medical term that did not exist during biblical times. Instead, the Bible uses other terms to describe the same condition.

> *The Spirit of the Sovereign LORD is on me, because the LORD has anointed me to preach good news to the poor. He has sent me to bind up the brokenhearted, to proclaim freedom for the captives and release from darkness for the prisoners, to proclaim the year of the Lord's favor and the day of vengeance of our God, to comfort all who mourn, and provide for those who grieve in Zion—to bestow on them a crown of beauty instead of ashes, the oil of gladness instead of mourning, and a garment of praise instead of a spirit of despair.*
>
> (Isaiah 61:1–3)

Here, the Bible calls depression the *"spirit of despair."* The King James Version calls it the *"spirit of heaviness."* When people are depressed, they often feel heavy. It feels as though a huge weight hangs around their necks. After praying for people with depression, I often hear them testify, "I feel light." That is a common description of the experience of being delivered from depression.

> *Satan attacks the mind above everything else; therefore, it is no surprise to find demons making people depressed.*

Depression is a condition of the mind. As we have learned, Satan attacks the mind above everything else; therefore, it is no surprise to find demons making people depressed. Depression is the leading mental health problem. More people check in to hospitals due to depression than any other single cause. There is an epidemic of depression.

Is It Really a Demon?

Some professionals may question whether depression is caused by demons or by a chemical imbalance in the brain. I don't pretend to be an expert in the field of psychiatry—I will leave that field to them, hoping that they won't pretend to be experts in theology. I am happy whenever a psychiatrist is able to help somebody. At the same time, it is clear from my experience that prayers for deliverance have also been effective in helping people with depression. My focus, therefore, will be on the spiritual side to overcoming depression.

In the Bible, King Saul has been a case study for those who are involved in the field of psychology. Some have diagnosed Saul with bipolar depression. They notice that he had all the symptoms of the illness. Yet, the Bible simply says that an evil spirit tormented him. Consider this: he would get relief when David played spiritual songs on his harp. It is clear that a spiritual focus helped to lift Saul's heaviness.

I think this is one way to tell whether an evil spirit is involved with the depression. If the depressed person feels better after focusing on the Lord, then it would seem to me that the problem is spiritual and not simply medical. On the other hand, if the person does not feel better after prayer or deliverance, then he may be suffering from a purely medical condition. In my experience, those who fall into the class of solely a medical condition are the minority. Most cases of depression are caused by something spiritual or mental.

God Draws Close

For when we came into Macedonia, this body of ours had no rest, but we were harassed at every turn—conflicts on the outside, fears within. But God, who comforts the downcast, comforted us by the coming of Titus. (2 Corinthians 7:5–6)

God is very close to those who are downcast. As much as a person feels that God has abandoned him, He is especially close to him. The Greek word in this verse for *"comfort"* means "to call to one's side, call for, summon."

When someone is feeling downcast, his depression actually calls God to come to his aid. This is the opposite of how it may feel to those who are downcast. They usually feel lonely, isolated, and all alone. But in the supernatural, God is closer to them than when they feel good.

> *If you are facing depression, remember, God is there beside you. He is close. You are not alone.*

Depression is the call for God to arrive on the scene. So, if you are facing depression, remember, God is there beside you. He is close. You are not alone. God is for you, and you will see brighter days ahead.

Do Not Refuse Comfort

There is a passage that speaks clearly to this subject, but it is also a warning. *"A voice is heard in Ramah, weeping and great mourning, Rachel weeping for her children and refusing to be comforted, because they are no more"* (Matthew 2:18).

It's possible for a person to refuse to be comforted. You may feel so sorry for yourself that you are convinced there is no help available for you. You tell yourself that nobody cares about you. Do you know what you are doing? You have become stubborn and are refusing to be comforted. Eventually, you will spiral down into a pit of depression.

In order to allow the Word of God to help you out of your depression, you must *listen* to the Word and *do* what it says.

Three Causes of Depression

I like to use the letters SAD as an acronym for the three causes of depression: Sin, Attitude, and, in the next chapter, Demons. We will discuss the first two causes in this chapter and the third in the next chapter.

Sin

In the course of time Cain brought some of the fruits of the soil as an offering to the LORD. But Abel brought fat portions from some of the firstborn of his flock. The LORD looked with favor on Abel and his offering, but on Cain and his offering he did not look with favor. So Cain was very angry, and his face was downcast. Then the LORD said to Cain, "Why are you angry? Why is your face downcast? If you do what is right,

133

will you not be accepted? But if you do not do what is right, sin is crouching at your door; it desires to have you, but you must master it." (Genesis 4:3–7)

This is the first case of depression recorded in the Bible, and the cause is plain: Cain sinned by not offering God an acceptable sacrifice. Consequently, God refused to accept his cheap gift. Cain became depressed when he saw his brother's gift being accepted by God. God then asked Cain a heart-probing question: *"Why is your face downcast?"* He wanted Cain to face the cause of his sadness.

Sometimes we may feel an unexplained sadness, and we can't pin down its origin. But if we are honest with ourselves, we may discover that, often, the reason for our depression is the fact that we went against our consciences and sinned. The solution is obvious: we need to repent.

In cases like this, no amount of time in therapy on a doctor's couch will provide much relief. We have sinned, and now we are facing the consequences. Or, perhaps we dislike ourselves. Sin depresses us. In either case, you don't need deliverance from an evil spirit. You need repentance.

A college student was depressed and suicidal because, in his opinion, his father was not giving him the approval he needed. The son told his counselor, "All my father does is complain about me."

The counselor asked, "Does he complain about your sister, too?"

"No, she is his favorite. She gets all the good grades. She gets all the awards at school."

The counselor wisely asked, "Is it true that she does well in school?"

"Yes, but what does that matter?"

"Well, I noticed that you are flunking two courses."

"So what?" he quipped. "My father has to accept me for who I am!"

The student's problem was not his father. The problem was his failure to do what was right, and now he had become depressed. You can't expect to be happy when you fail to do your best or to do what is right.

It is disappointing that many counselors do not act as wisely as that one did. Things have changed among psychiatrists. Many no longer emphasize the need to listen to one's conscience. Instead of suggesting ways in which their patients can improve their lives, they often commiserate with the depressed and misdiagnose them. In doing so, they reinforce the patients' behavior and continue the cycle of depression. You can't change your conscience; you can only submit to it.

For example, there was a time when the psychiatric field labeled homosexuality as a mental disorder. Now, through pressure from activists, professionals in the field of psychology have altered their opinion and treat it as a healthy alternative lifestyle. Despite the change in their diagnoses, the suicide rate for homosexual youth is two to three times higher than for heterosexual youth.[5] You can argue that they have been mistreated, maligned, or misunderstood, but I believe that their lifestyle is the underlying problem. There needs to be repentance.

> *The only answer to depression that comes as a result of sin is repentance.*

The same can be said about adultery. Of course people are depressed after they are caught in adultery. What would you expect? It is the consequence of sin. The only answer to depression that comes as a result of sin is repentance. There is no point in seeking spiritual deliverance if repentance is not the first step.

Attitude

Horrible circumstances can get anyone down. A death in the family, divorce, loss of income, or deteriorating health can all lead to depression. But there is hope for getting out of this kind of depression. The answer is in your attitude. Your attitude is based on the way you look at things.

[5] M. R. Feinlab, ed., "Prevention and Intervention in Youth Suicide," *Report of the Secretary's Task Force on Youth Suicide*, vol. 3 (1989).

As the old saying asks, "Do you see the glass as half *empty* or half *full*?" There is a lot to be said for optimism.

> *As Christians, we have an optimism based on a faithful God, not on some utopian fantasy.*

As Christians, we have an optimism based on a faithful God, not on some utopian fantasy. We believe that all things will work out for our good. (See Romans 8:28.) God has promised it. Our hope is based on God's faithfulness to His promises. King David knew this kind of hope.

> *As the deer pants for streams of water, so my soul pants for you, O God. My soul thirsts for God, for the living God. When can I go and meet with God? My tears have been my food day and night, while men say to me all day long, "Where is your God?" These things I remember as I pour out my soul: how I used to go with the multitude, leading the procession to the house of God, with shouts of joy and thanksgiving among the festive throng. Why are you downcast, O my soul? Why so disturbed within me? Put your hope in God, for I will yet praise him, my Savior and my God. My soul is downcast within me; therefore I will remember you from the land of the Jordan, the heights of Hermon—from Mount Mizar.*
>
> (Psalm 42:1–6)

David had just come back to the Lord after falling into sin with Bathsheba, the wife of another man. Despite his repentance, he still had to deal with the aftermath of his sin. God had forgiven him, but the people despised him, and he was losing their confidence. His kingdom was deteriorating. Even his son was conspiring against him. Things were bleak for David when he wrote this psalm. In it, he described his soul as being *"downcast within me."*

That is a good description of depression. You feel down. Your posture shows it. It is hard to look up; you talk to people with your eyes tilted downward.

How did David get out of this depression?

First, he truly repented of his past actions. *"My soul pants for you, O God."* He was thirsty to know more of God. Despite his failure, he had made a 180-degree about-face.

Second, he poured out his soul to God. *"Men say to me all day long, 'Where is your God?' These things I remember as I pour out my soul."* Do not keep your depression hidden from God. He already knows about it; you might as well tell Him how you feel. When you do, you'll feel much better.

Third, David faced the real reason why he was depressed: he had lost hope in God. *"Why are you downcast, O my soul? Why so disturbed within me? Put your hope in God, for I will yet praise him, my Savior and my God."* Be honest with yourself. Are you depressed because you have lost hope in God that things will turn out for good?

David chose to put in his hope in God. In doing so, he decided, *"I will yet praise him."* Praise is an antidote for this kind of depression.

Rejoice Always

Philippians 4:4 says, *"Rejoice in the Lord always. I will say it again: Rejoice!"* How often are you to rejoice? You know the answer: always!

You might say, "I don't feel like rejoicing." Paul didn't say, "Rejoice only if you feel like it." No! He said, *"Rejoice in the Lord always."* Obviously, God knows that you don't always feel like rejoicing. But you need to anyhow, because if you don't, you lose the strength to fight. *"The joy of the Lord is your strength"* (Nehemiah 8:10).

James 1:2 says, *"Consider it pure joy, my brothers, whenever you face trials of many kinds."* Pure joy is not happiness. *Happiness* comes from the word *happen*. Happiness, therefore, is based on what is happening. If something good

> **God knows that you don't always feel like rejoicing. But you need to anyhow, because if you don't, you lose the strength to fight.**

is happening, you are happy. However, God says that pure joy occurs even in the midst of trials—when your car breaks down, when your kids get sick, when your boss cuts your hours, or when your spouse is in a bad mood.

Why did James tell us to consider it pure joy whenever we face trials? Because joy gives us strength to face our trials—and if we face our trials, we will overcome. James continued, *"The testing of your faith develops perseverance. Perseverance must finish its work so that you may be mature and complete, not lacking anything"* (verses 3–4). James believed he had victory over trials rather than merely accepting them.

"Yet I Will Rejoice"

I love Habakkuk 3:17:

Though the fig tree does not bud and there are no grapes on the vines, though the olive crop fails and the fields produce no food, though there are no sheep in the pen and no cattle in the stalls....

It certainly seems like Habakkuk had his share of problems. But look at the next verse.

...yet I will rejoice in the LORD, I will be joyful in God my Savior. (verse 18)

Yet! Yet! Yet! Notice, he was not willing to surrender to his problems. He was going to do something about them. Then, he added the reason he was able to rejoice:

The Sovereign LORD is my strength; he makes my feet like the feet of a deer, he enables me to go on the heights.

(Habakkuk 3:19)

Habakkuk had no intention of staying defeated. He may have *looked* defeated, but he was not going to *stay* defeated. The difference between the defeated person and the victorious person is not their circumstances but their attitudes.

An attitude of gratitude will put you over the top in life. This is the attitude Habakkuk had. Even when nothing good was happening in his life—no fruit, no crops, no sheep, no cattle—yet he rejoiced.

In our modern world, Habakkuk might have said it this way: "Though there is no food in the refrigerator and no money in the checking account, though the sickness gets worse and the pain persists, though my children are on drugs and my spouse does not appreciate me, yet I will rejoice in the Lord and be joyful in God my Savior!"

Regardless of your circumstances, you can still rejoice!

Once you eliminate the first two reasons for depression—sin and a negative attitude—then, you are ready to deal with any demons that may be causing your depression.

Chapter Ten

Deliverance from Demonic Depression

Derek Prince (1915–2003) seemed to have everything going for him. He had a good education, made decent money, and practiced upright morals. He was saved and began pastoring a church near the center of London, England. From every outward appearance, he was a successful minister. Each week in his church, he would witness at least one conversion or miracle of healing. Yet, he had an inner feeling of disappointment.

He felt an inaudible voice whispering to him, *Others may succeed, but you won't.* He could not shake the inner sense of grayness in his soul that seemed to match the gray surroundings of London. The skies were gray. The houses were gray. The people even seemed gray. Worse, Derek Prince's soul was gray.

He tried every means to get rid of his depression. He faithfully read his Bible. He fasted once a week. He devoted himself to days and weeks of intense prayer and fasting. Yet, despite all of his efforts, he never felt any better. He began to grow hopeless over his situation.

His answer came in 1953. He was reading the first part of Isaiah 61 when the phrase *"the spirit of heaviness"* (verse 3 KJV) forcefully struck his consciousness. There it was in Scripture—his condition. He had a spirit of heaviness in his life. He thought to himself, *Could it be that the force I am struggling with is not a part of me but an actual alien being?* He recalled the term *"familiar spirits"* (Leviticus 19:31 KJV). Could it be that a "familiar spirit" had attached itself to members of his family and had finally moved down to him?

He recalled his father's bout with depression. For the most part, he had behaved like a gentleman, but there had been rare times when something would upset him so much, he would shut out his family. For twenty-four hours, he would sit in stone silence. Then, for no apparent reason, he would return to his normal self.

After reading the passage from Isaiah, Derek Prince had a new revelation. He no longer viewed his depression as a part of his personality. He saw it as a demon that had come to make his ministry ineffective. The only issue now was how to deal with this spirit. He remembered Joel 2:32, *"And it shall come to pass, that whosoever shall call on the name of the LORD shall be delivered"* (KJV), and quickly put the passage into practice. He prayed, "Lord, You've shown me that I have been oppressed by a spirit of heaviness, but You also promised in Your Word that if I call on Your name, I shall be delivered. So I'm calling on You now to deliver me, in the name of Jesus."

No sooner did he utter this prayer than he felt something like a gigantic vacuum cleaner come down over him and suck away the gray mist around him. While this went on, he also felt a pressure in his chest forcefully release.

God came through and delivered Derek Prince, who described the experience with these words:

> Suddenly everything around me seemed brighter. I felt as if a heavy burden had been lifted from my shoulders. I was free![6]

A Demon of Depression

You may relate to Derek Prince's experience. Perhaps you, too, have an unexplained depression. You do not have any hidden sin that has not been confessed. Your situation is stable—nothing

[6]Derek Prince, *They Shall Expel Demons* (Grand Rapids, MI: Chosen Books [a division of Baker Book House], 1998), 33.

terrible has gone wrong with your life—yet, the depression remains and is real.

This depression causes you to become pessimistic. You lose any sense of excitement or optimism about the future. You feel everything is about to go wrong with your life.

You are depressed, and, in your case, it is demonic. Call on the Lord and watch what God can do for you. Your deliverance may not be as dramatic as that of Derek Prince, but it will be just as real. You might need to have someone pray deliverance over you, or you might have the faith to pray alone. God is sovereign! He can do it with or without other people praying for you.

Recently, a doctor in my church was suffering from depression. He could not explain why it was happening to him. He had everything anyone could ever want. Then, one day, he heard me teaching on the topic of deliverance. Immediately, he realized his problem was a demon. He had never thought a demon could attack him. After some prodding from his friends, he came forward for prayer. He sobbed as I laid hands on him. I spoke to the spirit of heaviness and commanded it to leave him. In that moment, he was freed. His wife told me that ever since that prayer, he has not suffered from depression.

Hope as a Helmet

Once you are delivered, do not let down your guard. Satan will try to return. In Derek Prince's case, he had to fight off many more attacks by the enemy. Over time, however, Satan eventually gave up. Demons will try to come back after deliverance. If the devil can trick you into believing that God has not delivered you, then he can bring his evil spirits back into your life. Therefore, you need to take a stand against the enemy.

> *Demons will try to come back after deliverance.*

Put on *"the hope of salvation as a helmet"* (1 Thessalonians 5:8). A helmet covers your head—your mind. You can suffer an injury to most parts of your body, but a head injury is often the most severe. The most important piece of equipment in any contact sport is the headgear. The same is true spiritually. You must protect your mind. And according to Scripture, the weapon God has provided for your mind is hope.

Hope is the positive expectation that God will work out His good plan for your life. You can tell when someone is hopeful. He watches with great expectation for his answer. If he is waiting for an important letter, he watches out the window for the mail delivery. If he is waiting for a loved one to call, he sits by the phone, expecting every call to be from that person.

When you are hopeful, you expect every day to be a miracle. You think, *Somehow, God is coming through for me.* If you are sick, you attend a miracle healing service. You don't stay home and say, "I probably won't get healed." No, when you are hopeful, you attend, expecting a miracle.

Chapter Eleven

Overcoming the Spirit of Jealousy

Keep all the doors to demons closed. Remember King Saul, who suffered from *"a tormenting spirit that filled him with depression and fear"* (1 Samuel 16:14 TLB)? A closer look at the story reveals an open doorway for a particular demon: jealousy.

Saul was a handsome man whom the people adored. He was *"an impressive young man without equal among the Israelites—a head taller than any of the others"* (1 Samuel 9:2). If ever there was someone who did not need to be jealous, it was Saul.

Later in his reign, a young man named David appeared, killed the giant Philistine, Goliath, and led Israel on triumphant invasions against their enemies. David had earned such an impressive reputation in Israel that young women danced and sang, *"Saul has slain his thousands,*

and David his tens of thousands" (1 Samuel 18:7).
This "hit song" did not sit well with King Saul.

> *Saul was very angry; this refrain galled him. "They have credited David with tens of thousands," he thought, "but me with only thousands. What more can he get but the kingdom?" And from that time on Saul kept a jealous eye on David.* (verses 8–9)

Saul's jealousy made him susceptible to the presence of demons.

> *The next day an evil spirit from God came forcefully upon Saul. He was prophesying in his house, while David was playing the harp, as he usually did. Saul had a spear in his hand and he hurled it, saying to himself, "I'll pin David to the wall." But David eluded him twice.* (verses 10–11)

Notice the correlation between Saul's jealousy and the evil spirit. Evil spirits feed on jealousy.

The Idol of Jealousy

> *He stretched out what looked like a hand and took me by the hair of my head. The Spirit lifted me up between earth and heaven and in visions of God he took me to Jerusalem, to the entrance to the north gate of the inner court, where the idol that provokes to jealousy stood.* (Ezekiel 8:3)

As we discussed in chapter two, an idol is a demon. (See also 1 Corinthians 10:20.) Demons can provoke jealousy. This is what happened with Saul. He allowed the temptation of jealousy to lodge in his soul, and, consequently, an evil spirit was able to enter and torment him, which caused him to attack David. I have seen this duplicated in the lives of many people.

When people are confronted with the sin of jealousy, they usually deny it. "What? Me, jealous? You've got to be kidding. Why would I possibly be jealous of her?" There is good reason why people usually deny having jealousy. They deny it because they do not actually know what it is. There is a widespread misconception regarding this sin.

Jealousy does not imply inferiority. A person who is jealous does not feel the least bit inferior to the person he is jealous of. The Bible says, *"I, the* LORD *your God, am a jealous God"* (Exodus 20:5), and we know God does not feel inferior to anyone. Jealousy is a right that only God can claim. God can be jealous because no one is better or greater than He is. We can't say that about ourselves. No one else has the right to be jealous.

Jealousy is not an emotion. It's not like fear or depression. We know how those conditions feel because fear and depression have their own emotions. When we fear, we might become nervous or feel a knot in the pit of our stomachs. We know

> **Jealousy does not have its own emotion. This is why it is hard to pinpoint when you have it.**

what fear feels like. Similarly, when we are depressed, we feel down, discouraged, and empty, and our faces show it. There are other emotions, such as guilt and resentment, that have distinct feelings. But jealousy does not have its own emotion. This is why it is hard to pinpoint when you have it.

While jealousy is not an emotion, it is able to produce emotions. Rather than producing its own emotion, it *borrows* other emotions. For example, no one would dispute the fact that Cain was jealous of his brother, Abel. Look at this passage:

> *But Abel brought fat portions from some of the firstborn of his flock. The LORD looked with favor on Abel and his offering, but on Cain and his offering he did not look with favor. So Cain was very angry, and his face was downcast.* (Genesis 4:4–5)

Later, Cain murdered his brother. It is clear that the root of Cain's problem was jealousy, but the Bible never uses this word to describe Cain. Instead, the Bible describes a certain emotion that Cain felt: anger. It tells us that his facial expression was downcast. There is no mention, however, of jealousy. This is because jealousy is the root of many negative emotions, such as anger, depression, fear, anxiety, and resentment. The emotions were obvious in Cain, but God wanted him to recognize them—as well as their source.

"Why are you angry? Why is your face downcast?" (Genesis 4:6). Instead of accusing Cain of being angry and depressed, God asked him *why* he was angry and depressed. Cain knew he was angry. He also recognized the fact that he was depressed. But God wanted Cain to face the reason for these emotions. It was fairly obvious: Cain was jealous of his brother, Abel. By not facing the cause of his emotional problems, he started down the path of destruction.

The same was true of King Saul. He never faced the reason for his resentment of David. David had not done anything wrong to Saul. He had served the king faithfully. David never conspired against him, yet Saul hated him. Why? He hated David because he was jealous.

"The Spirit...Lusteth to Envy"

Are you beginning to see something about jealousy, perhaps even in your own life? Jealousy affects every kind of relationship, whether it's between spouses, siblings, coworkers, or fellow church members. It can wreck good relationships. It wrecked the relationships between Joseph and his brothers, between Rachel and

Leah, and between Jacob and Esau. Jealousy has even been the cause of wars.

> *What causes fights and quarrels among you? Don't they come from your desires that battle within you? You want something but don't get it. You kill and covet, but you cannot have what you want.* (James 4:1–2)

Jealousy is based on coveting what another person has. Coveting is the sin of jealousy. James added, *"Do ye think that the scripture saith in vain, The spirit that dwelleth in us lusteth to envy?"* (verse 5 KJV). The *"spirit...lusteth to envy."* This evil spirit causes us to envy.

In Scripture, it is clear that an evil spirit can cause both envy and jealousy.

Envy is another word for *jealousy*. Technically, they are different. Envy usually involves only two parties—you want what someone else has. Jealousy can involve more than two parties. For instance, you may become jealous because someone else has "stolen" the affection of the one you love. In the Hebrew text, there is only one word for both *jealousy* and *envy: qana'*. In Scripture, it is clear that an evil spirit can cause both envy and jealousy.

The modern-day Israeli and Palestinian conflict is primarily due to jealousy. Both groups feel entitled to have more than the other group. Jealousy was also the root reason why the temple leaders wanted Christ crucified. We can never underestimate the power of jealousy.

A woman once made arrangements with an artist to sit for a portrait. She told the artist, "Although I have only a few items of jewelry, nevertheless, I want this painting to show me wearing diamond rings and earrings, an emerald brooch, and a multi-strand necklace of pearls that look like they are priceless."

"I can do this," said the artist, "but do you mind telling me why you want this when it is apparent that you do not particularly care for jewelry?"

The woman replied, "If I die first and my husband remarries, I want his second wife to go out of her mind trying to find where I hid all of my jewels."

> *Because it can remain hidden, jealousy must be diagnosed early, or it will stay undetected and cause wounds that cannot be easily healed.*

We laugh at this joke, but jealousy is no laughing matter. It ruins families, businesses, churches, and even governments. It will torment your soul like nothing else can. Worse, in most cases, you won't even know that you have it. It is a hidden disease.

Jealousy: A Threefold Definition

Because it can remain hidden, jealousy must be diagnosed early, or it will stay undetected and cause wounds that cannot be easily healed. How can you tell if you are sick with jealousy? It would help if you understood what jealousy is. I have three definitions of jealousy.

1. The Fear of Losing Love

The first definition of jealousy is the fear of losing the love, affection, or favor of someone else. For instance, suppose that you are the lead vocalist in the praise and worship team at your church. One day, someone more talented than you joins the team. Your position is suddenly threatened. Instead of being happy for your church that other talented singers are joining the team, you begin to look for faults with the new singer and subtly point them out to the pastor or worship leader.

"She doesn't seem spiritual enough."

"He shows up late."

"She seems to have too much pride."

What is happening here? Jealousy is manifesting as fear, which causes you to do whatever you can to hold on to your position of esteem.

2. Anger at What Someone Else Has

The second definition of jealousy is experiencing anger, unhappiness, or depression due to what someone else has. For instance, suppose your neighbor buys a new luxury automobile. As he pulls into his driveway, you put on your best smile and tell him how much you like his car. But, secretly, you are not happy. You look at your own car and feel dissatisfaction. It suddenly seems so outdated. You no longer enjoy driving.

Now, suppose the owner of the new car is your pastor. You grow angry over his purchase and are quick to tell others how he is wasting his money on a lavish lifestyle. Subtly—or maybe not so subtly— you begin to turn other church members against him.

Or, what if your son tries out for the local Little League team and does not make the cut, but your best friend's son makes it? How do you feel about your friend's son? Are you truly happy for him, or do you think, *His son is no better than mine. If he made the team, my son definitely should have made it.* Things are different the next time you have dinner with your best friend. You no longer seem to enjoy his company.

What is taking place in these scenarios?

Your jealousy is manifesting as unhappiness over what someone else has or accomplishes. As a result, you begin to dislike that person.

3. Anxiety about Keeping What You Have

The third definition of jealousy is defensively guarding your possessions or relationships. For instance, you begin to believe that another woman has an eye for your husband. Suddenly, you can't stand her. Your husband takes you out for a romantic evening at a new restaurant that you've wanted to go to for months, but when you are seated, you notice that "other woman" across the dining room. "Why is she here?" you angrily ask your husband. Are you able to enjoy your meal, or are you seething over the presence of this other woman? You are angry because of an irrational fear of losing your husband. The evening is ruined.

What has happened? Your jealousy has manifested as a desire to guard your husband. You become overprotective. You may pretend it is because you care for him, but, in reality, you yourself are the cause of your concern.

The issue of jealousy can occur in the lives of pastors, as well. One pastor schedules an important event at his church, only to discover that another church is holding an even larger event. The pastor begins to make sly remarks to certain members of the congregation about the carnality of "certain churches." Because of jealousy, this pastor becomes afraid of losing congregants to the other church. He may think he is only showing concern for his congregation, but, in reality, he is more concerned about his own ministry.

Tragic Effects of Jealousy

The Bible warns us of the tragic effects that jealousy will have on our lives. *"A heart at peace gives life to the body, but envy rots the bones"* (Proverbs 14:30).

You can ruin your health by allowing jealousy to rule your life. Our bones are essential for our health. They contain marrow that produces new blood cells. If your bones are rotting, your health is deteriorating. Here is another warning:

> *You can ruin your health by allowing jealousy to rule your life.*

"Resentment kills a fool, and envy slays the simple. I myself have seen a fool taking root, but suddenly his house was cursed" (Job 5:2–3).

Does it ever seem that whenever life is going well, something awful suddenly happens? You don't understand why God would allow it. Little do you realize that *"envy slays the simple."* Everything seemed so "rooted," but suddenly, your house feels cursed. It may be because of jealousy.

How many times have we seen successful people who seemed invincible brought down in a matter of seconds? They seemed so rooted. Their problems seemed to come out of nowhere. Few realize that the secret cause of their downfall was jealousy.

Overcoming Jealousy

Do not let your heart envy sinners, but always be zealous for the fear of the LORD.

There is surely a future hope for you, and your hope will not be cut off.
(Proverbs 23:17–18)

In order to overcome jealousy, it is important that we know *"the fear of the LORD."* This means that we recognize the fact that God is watching the way we treat others. It's hard to avoid certain emotions when others receive blessings, or when you feel as though your position is being threatened. You are human; you will experience fear, depression, and even anger. But you must not act on these emotions, either in word or in deed. Do not speak evil of others when they are blessed. Rejoice with them, instead. Make it your purpose to live in a right way with others. Remember, *"There is surely a future hope for you, and your hope will not be cut off."* God has a great plan for you, as well as for others. He blesses others because He loves them. When He does, do not think that He has forgotten you.

Pastors, your churches will grow in God's time. Fathers, your children will find their talents. Wives, God will protect your husbands without your help. If things do not turn out as planned, rest assured, God has something better for you. You do not need to become discouraged when it seems that God has passed you by—He has not. He will still bless you. You do not need to *envy* anyone. Ask God for deliverance from your jealousy, and He will rescue you.

Chapter Twelve

Dealing with Anger

Marlene had a personality disorder. One of the manifestations of this disorder was that any small problem would trigger an angry outburst. She blew up at almost anything. People were afraid to be around her. She was working with a television crew at a large meeting I held in Houston. During the meeting, the Holy Spirit began to touch her through my teaching and prayers for the people. Even as she captured the many miracles taking place for the broadcast, she was receiving her own miracle. In a moment—an instant of time—she was delivered from her anger. She later wrote to me to testify of her miracle. Since that meeting, she claims that she has been mostly free from angry outbursts.

You may wonder, *Why wasn't she "completely" freed from her anger?*

We are not supposed to be *completely* free from anger. Unlike most other mental issues, anger is not always bad or harmful. There are instances when God gives us permission to be angry. *"Be ye angry, and sin not"* (Ephesians 4:26 KJV). God understands our inborn capacity for anger. As beings created in God's image, we tend to exhibit God's personality. If God gets angry from time to time, then it is not always wrong for us to experience anger, either.

> *If God gets angry from time to time, then it is not always wrong for us to experience anger, either.*

Jesus threw the money changers out of the temple after making a whip to help get the job done. (See John 2:13–16.) I doubt He did so with a smile on His face. Yet, during an earlier episode of anger, Jesus was able to heal a man at the same time.

> *Another time* [Jesus] *went into the synagogue, and a man with a shriveled hand was there. Some of* [the Pharisees] *were looking for a reason to accuse Jesus, so they watched him closely to see if he would heal him....*[Jesus] *looked around at them in anger and, deeply distressed at their stubborn hearts, said to the man, "Stretch out your hand." He stretched it out, and his hand was completely restored.*
>
> (Mark 3:1–2, 5)

What Jesus was feeling is sometimes called "righteous indignation." This is the anger one experiences as a result of injustice against others or against God. While it is appropriate to feel anger when you see others mistreated or when God is being maligned, our problem is that we tend to feel anger toward injustice mostly when it is leveled at us.

MADD (Mothers Against Drunk Driving) is an organization that was founded by a mother whose daughter was killed by a drunk driver. She did not want others to go through what she went through, so, instead of languishing in anger against the one who took her daughter's life, she channeled her anger and founded an organization that lobbies lawmakers for tougher laws against those who drink and drive. Who knows how many lives her angry energy has saved?

If you try to suppress anger, it will generally only make you angrier. In his book *Make Anger Your Ally*, Neil Clark Warren wrote,

> Anger is completely natural, perfectly legitimate. It is that internal happening which prepares us to cope with hurtful, frustrating, and fearful experiences....Anger is simply a state of physical readiness.[7]

---

[7]Neil Clark Warren, *Make Anger Your Ally* (Wheaton, IL: Tyndale House, 1990), 36.

Good anger leads us to readiness. Readiness leads us in a good direction. Jesus' good anger made Him ready to take on greed in the temple. Good anger sounds like "Ready, aim, fire!"

Bad anger, however, leads us in a direction in which things go from bad to worse. Bad anger sounds more like "Anger, rage, fury!" This kind of anger does not lead anywhere productive because it is self-absorbed. Instead of making us physically ready, it ruins our readiness by causing us to lose control of our actions. The apostle Paul called this type of anger *"fits of rage"* (Galatians 5:20) and *"outbursts of anger"* (2 Corinthians 12:20). The anger itself is not a sin; it is the loss of control that is the problem. It is in the expression of anger where sin occurs, not in the emotion of anger itself.

This is what happened when God rejected Cain's offering yet accepted the offering of his brother, Abel. Cain felt this was unfair and became angry.

> *Then the LORD said to Cain, "Why are you angry?...Sin is crouching at your door; it desires to have you, but you must master it."* (Genesis 4:6, 7)

Notice that Cain was angry *before* he sinned. At that time, according to God, sin was only at the door. Cain had not yet let it come into his life. This demonstrates that it is possible to feel the emotion of anger and not be sinning. You do not need to repent of anger. However, anger over feelings of personal injustice can bring sin to your door. God's command to Cain is clear: *"You must master it."* He did not say to get rid of it. You should not look to get rid of anger or to kill it. Instead, you must use it for the good of others and for God's kingdom.

Without proper anger, we lose a potential ally in our walk with God. We need anger, but we need to master it. Cain, of course, did not master his anger; he let it master him, and it led to the murder of his brother.

> *You should not look to get rid of anger or to kill it. Instead, you must use it for the good of others and for God's kingdom.*

Genghis Khan

Whenever Genghis Khan went hunting, he always had his faithful hunting hawk by his side. It flew high above Khan and circled the sky until it spotted potential game. Khan tracked and hunted many animals this way.

One hot summer day, according to legend, Khan was thirsty, and his water pouch was dry. In the distance, he heard the faint sound of a waterfall. He tracked its sound until he found a small stream of water, coming from a crevice at the top of a rocky hill, that flowed into a puddle of water at Khan's feet. He unpacked a metal cup and dipped it into the puddle of water. As he brought the cup to his mouth, however, the trusty hawk flew in and knocked it from his hand. He tried again to drink the water, but the hawk did the same thing. This made Khan angry. Once again, he dipped the cup into the water, but this time he held a sword in his hand. As he saw the hawk approach to knock the cup from his hand, he struck his beloved bird and killed it.

At first, Khan was delighted at having removed the pest, but then regret settled in. Why had his faithful hawk tried to keep him from drinking the water? Just then, Khan saw something strange at the mouth of the crevice from which the water flowed. He climbed the small hill, and there in the pool of water leading to the falls was a dead animal. The water coming from the hill had been contaminated by the carcass.

Khan ran back down the hill and fell to his knees beside his faithful hawk and wept. It was all because of his quick anger. Like Genghis Khan, we, too, get angry at the people who love us, often because they are telling us the truth or trying to help us avoid making mistakes in our lives.

Man's Anger versus God's Anger

"For man's anger does not bring about the righteous life that God desires" (James 1:20). James called bad anger *"man's anger."* This is

significant because he was differentiating between man's anger and God's anger. The difference between the two is the speed. Look at the previous verse: *"Everyone should be quick to listen, slow to speak and slow to become angry"* (James 1:19).

1. Man's anger is quick; God's anger is slow.

God's anger is a slow-burning anger. *"But you, O Lord, are a compassionate and gracious God, slow to anger, abounding in love and faithfulness"* (Psalm 86:15). The God of the Bible gets angry, but Scripture tells us that He is *"slow to anger."* This should be your aim. Learn to avoid quick reactions when you feel anger. Think first before you act. Thomas Jefferson loved to say, "Count to ten when you are angry." That was his way of saying, "Pause; don't do anything. Wait on it."

> *Learn to avoid quick reactions when you feel anger. Think first before you act.*

"In your anger do not sin; when you are on your beds, search your hearts and be silent" (Psalm 4:4). The issue is not anger but the sin that anger can produce. David, the author of this psalm, gave us some great advice: "Search your hearts and be silent." Be honest about your feelings and why you are angry. Is your anger justified? Is it personal? If it is personal, let it go. If it

is justified, think carefully about what you are about to do because of it. Perhaps you should do nothing.

I once became angry when a minister of another church offered a job to one of the leaders of my congregation. I thought it was not proper protocol. In my view, he should have asked me for permission first. My wife and I met with the minister and told him how disappointed and hurt we were that he had done this. He looked at me and said, "If put in the same situation, I would do it again. I have no problem taking members from your church." But there was more. "And, by the way," he added, "the trouble with you is you let your wife rule the church." Apparently this man did not believe that women should ever preach.

I became even more incensed. What did my wife have to do with anything? Obviously, that meeting did not end well. Afterward, I vowed to my wife, "I am going to write a letter to all the pastors who have worked with this man in the past to tell them what he did to us and warn them about his motives."

My dear wife—a peacemaker by nature—said, "Tom, I know he did wrong, but that is only going to make you look petty. In the end, people are not going to look up to you if you write a nasty letter."

Still burning, I said, "I am going to sit on this letter until my anger leaves. Then, when there is no more anger but only direction from the Lord, I will write it." After a few days, my anger subsided, and the desire to write the letter subsided, as well. *"A quick-tempered man does foolish things"* (Proverbs 14:17). By sitting on my anger, I avoided writing a foolish letter.

I wish I had been more patient early on in my ministry, but I had not yet learned to control my anger. On several occasions, I quickly acted on anger and humiliated some church members. I now realize that even though they were humiliated, I was the one who looked bad. There aren't many sins that actually make us look ugly, but anger is one that does. No one is pretty or handsome when he is angry.

> *There aren't many sins that actually make us look ugly, but anger is one that does. No one is pretty or handsome when he is angry.*

Over the years, the biggest personal strides I have made have been in the area of anger management. While I still have the hot temper of an Irishman, I have learned mostly to sit on it. My anger has also led me to some very positive actions, including leading a movement in our city to reverse the city council's decision to provide health benefits to the homosexual partners of city employees. Without anger over immorality, I would have sat on the sideline and would not have fought against injustice. You can never be a great leader until you have truly mastered anger.

"Better a patient man than a warrior, a man who controls his temper than one who takes a city" (Proverbs 16:32). Even in my fight with city hall, I had to control my temper. If I had not, I would have eventually hurt our cause. Showing kindness, strength, and patience at the same time brought credibility to our side.

When God was angry with Israel, He told Moses to go to the Promised Land without Him. He explained why. *"I will not go with you, because you are a stiff-necked people and I might destroy you on the way"* (Exodus 33:3). God understands the need to look away—or walk away—from the source of displeasure in order to prevent a destructive venting of anger. Sometimes, people think they should test themselves to see how much they can put up with. Here, however, God indicated He would simply walk away. There is a great lesson in this: sometimes, you need to remove yourself from the cause of your anger. It is not the coward's way out but a divine way to manage anger.

2. Man's anger is long; God's anger is short.

Not only is man's anger different from God's anger in terms of speed, but it is also different in terms of duration. Psalm 30:5 says, *"For his anger lasts only a moment, but his favor lasts a lifetime.*" God does not stay angry. In Scripture, whenever God was angry—and showed it through His discipline—it was intended only to bring "*his favor*" back into a person's life. It is okay to be angry at people, but you must express your anger only in a way that brings reconciliation. If you remain angry, you are not being Christlike.

> *It is okay to be angry at people, but you must express your anger only in a way that brings reconciliation.*

"*Do not let the sun go down while you are still angry*" (Ephesians 4:26). Failure to follow this advice has led many loving couples into divorce court. While it is normal and healthy for couples to express disappointment with each other, such expressions should not last more than a day. To the best of your ability, you must address the hard feelings between you, forgive, and then let go of the past.

The apostle Paul explained why you must not stay angry for long: "*Do not give the devil a foothold*" (Ephesians 4:27). Staying angry provides the devil with a foothold in marriages and other types of relationships. And when the devil gains that foothold, he will be able to bring other wicked things into the relationship. When you go to bed angry, you are sleeping with the enemy—and I mean the devil, not your spouse. For the devil, anger is as blood is to a lion. Like a lion, the devil looks for injured prey. When he finds an angry person, he moves in to devour the injured prey. You are at your weakest when you are angry.

It's normal to feel hurt when someone wrongs you, but you must act to address your wounds before infection sets in. Unfortunately, many people choose to remain angry, putting themselves at risk for infection to spread.

This is what the Lord says:

For three sins of Edom, even for four, I will not turn back my wrath. Because he pursued his brother with a sword, stifling all compassion, because his anger raged continually and his fury flamed unchecked.

(Amos 1:11)

There were several reasons why the kingdom of Edom lost God's favor, and among them was their constant, uncontrolled anger. Interestingly, God said that He would not turn back His wrath because Edom did not put a stop to their wrath. God's wrath was directed toward those whose wrath continued unaddressed.

3. Man's anger is destructive; God's anger is constructive.

In one heartbreaking case, a three-year-old boy found his father's hammer and, without knowing better, began to bang dents into his father's new truck. The father heard the noise and came out of the house to see what his child had done. He was so angry that he grabbed the same hammer and began to hit his son's hands with it, crushing the boy's fingers. Realizing what he had done, the father quickly rushed his son to the hospital. Sadly, the doctors could not save the boy's fingers.

With tears in his eyes, the father went to his son and said, "I am so sorry."

The little boy said, "It's okay, Daddy." Then, the boy cracked a faint smile, looked his daddy in the eyes, and asked, "Daddy, when will my fingers grow back?"

Man's anger destroys; God's anger restores. You know you have failed when your anger cannot restore what was lost. Man's anger will never bring about the righteous life God desires.

> *Man's anger destroys; God's anger restores.*

Steps to Managing Anger

1. Take responsibility for your anger.

Contrary to what you may think, no one can *make* you angry. Other people can tempt you, but they cannot force you to be angry. That is your choice.

Over the years, I have heard many excuses: "But this person would not shut up. I told him to be quiet, but he kept talking. What was I supposed to do?" Such an excuse is an example of the lies people tell themselves to justify their anger.

Even abused wives will make excuses for their violent husbands: "It's not really his fault. I provoked him." Here's the fact: no one can *make* anyone react violently. You must not excuse others—or yourself—from outbursts of anger.

*For as churning the milk produces butter,
and as twisting the nose produces blood,
so stirring up anger produces strife.*
(Proverbs 30:33)

If you keep churning milk, what do you get? You get butter. Physician and author Dr. Sam Peeples said, "The circumstances of life, the events of life, and the people around me in life, do not make me the way I am, but reveal the way I am."

If you keep stirring up an angry man, you will get strife. The fact that he becomes angry only proves the kind of person he is. But a self-controlled, patient man will not produce strife or inappropriate anger, no matter how much he is provoked.

An elderly man was at the grocery store with his grandson. The grandson was knocking over cans, stealing bites of fruit, and running wild throughout the store. Each and every time, the old man would calmly say, "Take it easy, Albert. Take it easy, Albert. I said, 'Take it easy, Albert.'"

A woman noticed how calm the grandfather was and could not help but congratulate him. "Sir, I have been watching you from the moment you entered the store with your grandson. I saw how unruly he was, yet you kept your cool and told him to take it easy. You never lost your temper." She looked at the little boy and said, "Albert, you are lucky to have such a patient grandfather."

The grandfather replied, "Thank you for your kindness. I do try to be patient. By the way, I'm Albert."

The lesson is clear: you cannot control other people, only yourself. Take responsibility for who you are and make the necessary changes within to alter what has been coming out.

2. Rectify the situation, if you can.

If something is bothering you, do your best to express to the person responsible what it is and what can be done. In other words, don't keep it a secret when something can be done to resolve the situation. If you keep it to yourself, you will grow angrier and angrier and unconsciously take that anger out on someone else.

Passive-aggressive people are known to do this. They show their anger through actions rather than express it through words. They shy away from healthy, direct confrontation, such as expressing a need or telling someone else how they were hurt by his actions. Instead, their anger leaks out in other, harmful ways. They may inadvertently forget to attend a party the other person invited them to, or they might consciously do something that offends the other party, all the while pretending that nothing is wrong. The passive-aggressive person does not appear to be angry, but his actions speak louder than words.

> *You are not judge, jury, and executioner. Let some things go and put your trust in God's justice.*

3. Put your trust in God's justice.

You may not always have the opportunity to let other people know that they did or said something to offend you. If so, what do you do? You must let God handle it. Don't try to seek revenge.

> *Do not take revenge, my friends, but leave room for God's wrath, for it is written: "It is mine to avenge; I will repay," says the Lord.* (Romans 12:19)

You are not judge, jury, and executioner. Let some things go and put your trust in God's justice.

I had to do this with the pastor who hired away one of my leaders. Instead of writing an angry letter to everyone who knew the man, I let it go and forgave him. I put the situation in God's hands. If what he did to me was wrong—and if he was continuing to do similar things to other pastors—then God would deal with him.

To my complete and utter shock, I eventually learned that this pastor died of a heart attack within two years of hiring that leader from my church. Please know that I did not rejoice at this man's passing, nor did I ever believe that his death was a consequence of his actions toward me or anyone else. I left the situation in God's hands, and I have to trust that His will was done.

4. Get a prayer partner who won't let you stay angry.

Do not make friends with a hot-tempered man, do not associate with one easily angered, or you may learn his ways and get yourself ensnared. (Proverbs 22:24–25)

Our associations greatly affect our moods. If you are prone to anger, the best person for you to associate with would be a calm prayer partner. In time spent with that person, you will learn his ways of patience.

> *It's not a coincidence that angry people seem to attract other angry people.*

It's not a coincidence that angry people seem to attract other angry people. Just as you can adopt the ways of hot-tempered folks by being around them, you can also learn the ways of coolheaded folks by associating with them.

This prayer partner can also help set you free from any demon that might be provoking the anger within you. If you feel another personality within you becoming angry, it might be a sign there is a demon present. Do whatever it takes to receive deliverance from the demon of anger.

5. Receive forgiveness for your past anger.

You may be reading this and experiencing strong conviction for allowing anger to possess your soul. We all make mistakes, but I believe that God forgives anger just as He forgives any other sin. So, confess your anger to God and let Him forgive you. Sometimes, you have to receive forgiveness for damage that cannot be repaired.

A little boy was suffering from a temper problem. So, his father had an ingenious idea to help his son understand the problem of anger. He gave the boy a bag of nails and said, "Whenever you have an outburst of anger, you have to take a nail and hammer it into the fence." The son agreed, and, for several weeks, he was constantly putting nails into the fence. Later, he began to notice that he was becoming angry less and less often. After months of doing this, he completely stopped experiencing any outbursts of anger.

"Dad, I have not grown angry in many weeks," he told his father. "What do you want me to do?"

"Son, you have learned your lesson. Now, go and pull out all the nails from the fence."

As he pulled out thirty-seven nails, the son looked bewildered. "Dad, there are so many holes in the fence. It looks ugly."

The father replied, "That is what anger does. You can be sorry for becoming angry, but the damage is done."

As I conclude this chapter, you may feel regret for the damage your anger has caused. However, God is merciful. Just as He wants you to be merciful to others, He will show mercy to you. Confess your sin to God, and He will be faithful to forgive you and to *cleanse* you from unrighteousness. (See 1 John 1:9.) He will not only forgive you, but, through your heartfelt confession, He will also cleanse you from the power of your anger.

Chapter Thirteen

God's Solution for Stress

Life can be stressful. It's difficult to juggle marriage and kids, especially if you are having problems in one or both areas. Marriage is tough enough without the additional stress of persistent arguments. And if you have problems with even one child, this can compound an already stressed-out life. Add to that the pressures of a career! With deadlines to make, customers to see, and your boss's expectations to meet, life can become too much to handle.

The Bible gives a practical and spiritual solution for stress:

Do not be anxious about anything, but in everything, by prayer and petition, with thanksgiving, present your requests to God. And the peace of God, which transcends all understanding, will guard your hearts and your minds in Christ Jesus.

Finally, brothers, whatever is true, whatever is noble, whatever is right, whatever is pure, whatever is lovely, whatever is admirable—if anything is excellent or praiseworthy—think about such things. Whatever you have learned or received or heard from me, or seen in me—put it into practice. And the God of peace will be with you.

(Philippians 4:6–9)

The message is simple: pray right, think right, and live right.

Pray Right

God cares about your life, and you can go to Him about every problem you face. Prayer, however, is more than just asking God for something. This Scripture says, *"But in everything, by prayer and petition, with thanksgiving, present your requests to God."*

Petition is part of prayer, but if it were the only part of prayer, why would this verse say *"prayer and petition"*? It is not enough to petition—you need to pray with thanksgiving, too.

Even Jesus' prayer began with acknowledging the greatness and holiness of God.

When Jesus taught us how to pray, He showed us that prayer begins not with asking for our daily bread but with praising God. *"Our Father in heaven, hallowed be your name"* (Matthew 6:9). Even Jesus' prayer began with acknowledging the greatness and holiness of God.

The nation of Judah once faced an insurmountable problem. Three nations had conspired together to annihilate them. King Jehoshaphat bowed down in prayer, and then, some Levite priests stood and praised the Lord. (See 2 Chronicles 20:18–19.) In that atmosphere of praise, God spoke to them and said, *"The battle is not yours, but God's"* (verse 15). When the battle came, the king sent men ahead of his army, singing praises to God. Scripture says that *"as they began to sing and praise, the Lord set ambushes against* [their enemies] *who were invading Judah, and they were defeated"* (verse 22). The secret to their victory was praise.

When you praise God, you are actually magnifying the Lord. Recently, my wife bought me some reading glasses to help me better see small print or to use when the light is not very bright. When I use them, the print on the page *seems* bigger. In reality, it is still the same size, but I can read the words more easily. The same is true with God. God is always big—omnipotent. But sometimes our eyes are not able to see how big God is. Praising God is like putting on reading glasses that magnify Him in our sight. It's time to praise God, and when we do, He will remove our stress.

It's okay to petition God. Ask Him for what you need. If your problem is at home, ask God to change the situation. If it is at work or has to do with money issues, ask Him to meet your specific need. There is nothing wrong with presenting your requests to God. (See Philippians 4:6.) *"You do not have, because you do not ask God"* (James 4:2). God would do amazing things if only we would ask Him.

There is nothing wrong with presenting your requests to God.

I feel such peace when I specifically ask God to do something because I have this assurance that He will grant my request. This brings my mind under control. Don't simply complain about your stress; do something about it by asking God for what you need. Do you think you would still have stress if God came through by solving your problem? Of course not. If you are stressed out over a lack of money, do you think you would feel less stress if you had more of it? Go ahead and ask God for more money.

Before the great English evangelist Smith Wigglesworth entered full-time ministry, he was a plumber and an avid believer. One day, he received a call to do some plumbing work for a wealthy woman. From the moment he arrived at her home, Wigglesworth had such joy, whistling and softly singing praises to God as he did his work. The woman was impressed by this and asked, "Why are you so happy?"

Wigglesworth answered, "This morning, my little girl woke up with a fever. So, I prayed the prayer of faith, laid hands on her, and, blessed be God, He healed her. Jesus said, *'Ask, and ye shall receive, that your joy may be full.'* My joy is full this morning because the Lord has answered my prayer." (See John 16:24 KJV.) Smith Wigglesworth preached the goodness of God to that dear lady, and, gloriously, she was saved.

Answered prayer gave Wigglesworth peace and joy. If he had not prayed for his daughter, he might have gone to that woman's house burdened by stress. But because God answered his prayer, he had peace. Ask boldly and watch God come through for you.

In everything, by prayer and petition, with thanksgiving, present your requests to God. (Philippians 4:6)

This passage also includes the phrase *"with thanksgiving."* This means that when you pray, you should have an "attitude of gratitude." You can pray often, but if you are ungrateful for your life, your prayers won't do you much good.

I have noticed that gratitude is a rare trait. Jesus also acknowledged this. After He healed ten lepers, only one of them came back to thank Him. Jesus rhetorically asked, *"Were not all ten cleansed? Where are the other nine?"* (Luke 17:17). That's the way it is today, also. Many who are blessed and helped by the Lord do not see how good God is to them.

For although they knew God, they neither glorified him as God nor gave thanks to him, but their thinking became futile.

(Romans 1:21)

> **A mind without gratitude to the Lord is defenseless against Satan.**

I have never met a patient in a mental institution who regularly practiced gratitude. It seems that the devil works more effectively on those who are ungrateful. The battle is in the mind. A mind without gratitude to the Lord is defenseless against Satan. Protect your mind from stress by counting your blessings. Be grateful to God for all He has done for you.

Think Right

The next step in overcoming stress, according to Philippians, also has to do with the mind.

Finally, brothers, whatever is true, whatever is noble, whatever is right, whatever is pure, whatever is lovely, whatever is admirable—if anything is excellent or praiseworthy—think about such things.

(Philippians 4:8)

Think about what things? Things that are *"praiseworthy"*! Stress is primarily a mental thing.

> *The weapons we fight with are not the weapons of the world. On the contrary, they have divine power to demolish strongholds. We demolish arguments and every pretension that sets itself up against the knowledge of God, and we take captive every thought to make it obedient to Christ.*
>
> (2 Corinthians 10:4–5)

I have read this Scripture many times, but recently, something new came to me. The word *"pretension"* struck me. We are told to *"demolish...every pretension."* Pretension is the act of pretending. Actors pretend to be people they are not. When you see a movie, you are watching fictitious characters. They are the inventions of writers, directors, and actors. They are not real people but only actors, role-playing on the silver screen. But just because they are not real—and you realize that—does not mean your emotions are not moved. In the movie *The Silence of the Lambs*, when psychopathic killer Hannibal Lecter preys on his victims, we *feel* the terror on the screen.

Our minds are like movie screens on which we play out scenes that terrify us. We need to realize that these scenes are only pretensions. They are not real. Unfortunately, many people are unable to differentiate between the pretensions in their minds and the truth of God's Word. Too often, they believe the pretensions are true, but they are not!

This is how the devil works. He gets us to think about things that cause us stress. In reality, of course, God has promised to be with us at all times. (See Deuteronomy 31:6.) He promises that everything will work out for our good. (See Romans 8:28.) He promises not to allow us to be tested beyond our endurance. (See 1 Corinthians 10:13.) He promises us a great future. (See Jeremiah 29:11.) Then why stress out? Since we know that God is on our side (see Romans 8:31), there is no reason to allow a fantasy movie to be played out in our minds. We need to quit dwelling on the lies of the enemy.

> *Since we know that God is on our side, there is no reason to allow a fantasy movie to be played out in our minds.*

Live Right

Whatever you have learned or received or heard from me, or seen in me—put it into practice. And the God of peace will be with you. (Philippians 4:9)

After praying right and thinking right, you must finally *"put it into practice"* by living right. I love that! And who will be with you? The God of peace will be with you.

Perhaps you've heard the phrase "God be with you." Do you know what that actually means? It means that God will cause you to be success-ful. Whenever the Bible says that God was *with* someone, it refers to something God was doing for that person. How would you like God to work on your behalf? When God is working for you, you cannot fail.

Stress is an emotion of fear caused by the feeling that the worst will happen. However, if God is with you, the worst cannot happen. How can you get the God of peace to be with you? Practice the Word of God. There is no point in trying to get around the impor-tance of right living when it comes to overcoming stress.

> *Much of our stress is caused by wrong living.*

Much of our stress is caused by wrong living. A man who has an adulterous affair feels incred-ible stress as he tries to keep the affair secret. When the phone rings at home, his heart skips a beat, fearful that it's his mistress calling. He spends much time stressing and worrying about being found out.

A woman who broke the law now worries that she will be caught, fined, or even put in pris-on. Why break the law when all it does is stress you out?

Across the border from my city of El Paso, Texas, is Juarez, Mexico. You probably have heard of the mass killings that have taken place in Juarez over the past few years. Most of the killings were due to the cartels fighting for domination over the lucrative illegal drug market. What gets me is that they do this so they can have lots of money, drive fancy cars, and build multimillion-dollar mansions. For what? To live confined like prisoners in those mansions? They are afraid to go out for fear that an enemy will kill them or that someone will recognize them and call the police. Even in the security of their compounds, they worry that someone close to them will turn them in to the authorities for a reward.

It's insanity! Why sell your soul for all that money when you can't even enjoy it? It's stupid to live that way.

You don't have to be a criminal to live with constant stress. You can disobey God in many ways and find that your disobedience brings about needless worry. Even if you do something that does not bring punishment in this life, doing wrong still results in the stress of a guilty conscience. Is it worth all that stress?

God has the solution for stress. Read Philippians 4:6–9 again, slowly and meditatively. Ask God to show you how to practice this passage. Then, do it, and live a life free from stress.

Chapter Fourteen

What Causes Homosexuality?

A woman called and pleaded over the phone for me to preside over her brother's funeral. "Pastor Brown, even though my brother Juan[8] did not live in El Paso, he loved your ministry. He listened to your tapes, read your books, and absolutely loved the way you preached the Word. He knew his funeral was going to be in El Paso, so before he died, he told me that he did not want anyone but you to perform the funeral. So, please, would you do it?" Her pleadings touched my heart, so I agreed.

At the funeral, I gave my usual sermon on heaven and afterward opened up the podium for family members and friends to share their memories of the deceased. A very thin, frail-looking man—about the age of Juan—came forward to share. He mentioned that Juan had always

---

[8]Not his real name.

preached about Jesus and the need to be born again. At first, this man had refused to get saved, but through Juan's constant encouragement, he had eventually given his heart to Christ. Then, the man shocked me. He mentioned that he and Juan had been partners and had lived together in the same house for twenty years.

My eyebrows lifted. As I panned the room, I noticed several men about Juan's age sitting by themselves. As different people came forward, there was no mention of Juan's sexual orientation, only how much Juan loved the Lord. But it was clear that Juan also was gay.

I share this story because this chapter is written for all of the Juans in the church. It is my goal in this chapter to reach out to those of you who may be struggling with homosexual feelings and perhaps have even acted on them, yet are not looking to justify the sin or to be gullible by allowing gay activists to rewrite the Bible to rationalize your behavior. You know full well that the Bible disapproves of your lifestyle, but despite your desire to change, you can't seem to conform yourself to the holy standard of the Bible.

Is It Natural?

The Old Testament includes plenty of instances where homosexuality is condemned. Here is one passage: *"Do not lie with a man as one lies* with a woman; that is detestable" (Leviticus 18:22). The word *detestable* is one of the strongest words in the Hebrew language when it comes to condemnation. It does not mean that the action is merely wrong; it conveys the idea of polluting oneself. There are sins that we commit and can easily stop, but then there are

> *There are sins that we commit and can easily stop, but then there are sins that pollute us.*

sins that pollute us. Homosexuality is the type of sin that, according to the Old Testament, can pollute your life and darken your moral judgment.

The apostle Paul may have had this in mind when he wrote these strong words against homosexuality:

> *Therefore God gave them over in the sinful desires of their hearts to sexual impurity for the degrading of their bodies with one another. They exchanged the truth of God for a lie, and worshipped and served created things rather than the Creator—who is forever praised. Amen. Because of this, God gave them over to shameful lusts. Even their women exchanged natural relations for unnatural ones. In the same way the men also abandoned natural relations with women and were inflamed with lust for one another. Men committed indecent acts with*

other men, and received in themselves the
due penalty for their perversion.
(Romans 1:24–27)

In this passage, Paul used the phrase *"natural relations"* to refer to heterosexuality. By contrast, it would follow that homosexuality would be considered "unnatural."

Sexual relations between two men—or two women—is unnatural because, in the end, they will never be able to produce a baby. People can wave signs, protest state laws, and march for gay rights, but nothing they do will make an unnatural act become natural.

In the very beginning, God made a simple yet profound statement about the human race: *"So God created man in his own image, in the image of God he created him; male and female he created them"* (Genesis 1:27). The most fundamental fact of creation is that God made us *"male and female."* Only a male and female together can produce children. No amount of protest will change this fundamental fact.

According to Jesus, not only are a man and woman the only ones able to produce children, but also, they are the only ones who can be married.

"Haven't you read," he replied, "that at the beginning the Creator 'made them male and female,' and said, 'For this reason a man will

leave his father and mother and be united to his wife, and the two will become one flesh'? So they are no longer two, but one. Therefore what God has joined together, let man not separate."   (Matthew 19:4–6)

God is the performer of marriage. A judge may arrogantly think he can overrule what God has made, but he can't. A judge may declare that two men are married, but they will never be truly married. No judge is able to change nature—what God has created.

> *God made you to be healthy and whole, and any deviation from God's sexual standard is a symptom of a sickly person.*

I do not mean to sound harsh, but let's get real. Let's quit playing games with our sexual selves. Understand that God made you to be healthy and whole, and that any deviation from God's sexual standard is a symptom of a sickly person. Homosexuality is a deviation from the order God established.

Are Homosexuals Born or Made?

Someone may insist, "I was born this way; thus, God made me like this." People assume that they are born with only godly feelings. Since the fall of man, we have been born in sin with a corrupted nature that leads us into sinful life-styles. Simply because you have felt from youth

195

that you were born gay is not a sign that God made you that way. It is only further evidence that you were born a sinner. *"Surely I was sinful at birth, sinful from the time my mother conceived me"* (Psalm 51:5).

Even if it could be proven that genetics play a part in homosexuality, it would not prove that such a lifestyle is absolutely and indelibly the product of genetic predisposition. Genetics play an important role in shaping the kind of people we become, but other things—such as environment and the choices we make—also serve to shape our development. We are not doomed to be the products only of our genetics. We are also products of the choices we make.

Again, some may say, "But I did not choose to be a homosexual. I was born this way." According to gay activists, homosexuals are born the way they are, and there is no way for them to change. It would be like forcing left-handed people to use their right hands. It is the way they are born; they can't help it. These arguments are used to persuade society that any attempts to change the behavior of homosexuals are unreasonable, intolerant, and quite impossible.

Studies have been conducted in an attempt to find a so-called "gay gene," but to no avail. In my view, this search will never succeed be-cause if a "gay gene" existed, then the incidence of homosexuality would be decreasing due to the fact that homosexuals are not able to procreate and thus do not pass on the "gay gene." It seems, however, that homosexuality is on the rise. Of course, our society has only recently begun measuring the percentage of practicing homosexuals, but there is evidence that the number of homosexuals in society is increasing.

All the evidence I have seen shows that homosexuality is actually an emotional and psychological disorder brought on in early childhood. I do not believe people choose those feelings, because who in his right mind would do so and risk being scorned and ridiculed by society? I do not believe homosexuals initially choose their orientation any more than heterosexuals choose theirs.

An exception to this would be people who practice homosexuality out of convenience. This would include prisoners, students at same-sex schools, and men who find that far more men than women are willing to have sex with them. A church member once confided in me that he had engaged in several homosexual encounters over the years, yet he preferred women. When I asked him why he did it, he said, "It's easier to find men willing to do it than women." He went on to explain that there are men who are basically heterosexual who frequent gay establishments because they know they will get sex.

As aware as I am that there are those who practice homosexuality out of choice, I am writing to those who feel a natural and permanent desire to be with people of the same gender. For most, if it were their choice, they would choose to be heterosexuals in order to avoid the scorn of society.

I have been heterosexual for as far back as I can remember. I never *chose* those feelings. They were simply my psychological response to a normal, healthy childhood. Not everyone, however, experienced a normal, healthy childhood. When dramatic events happen in the lives of children, it can affect their psyches. Many of us are well aware of how certain vivid experiences still affect us to this day.

For example, as a child, I developed a fear of dogs that has never quite left me. I remember trick-or-treating at Halloween as a boy. One year, my sister, my best friend, and I went to a house where the back porch light was on, so we assumed that the back door was open for trick-or-treaters. I will never forget the moment when we opened the gate to knock on the door and several ferocious-sounding dogs charged at us from out of nowhere. Quickly, we leaped over the fence to avoid them, but my best friend did not quite make it. One of the dogs bit him on his calf. He started screaming, and blood was gushing from the wound. Later, at the hospital, he had to endure more than one hundred stitches. This event haunted me for years. Ever since then, I have struggled with a fear of dogs. Eventually, I won the battle, but even to this day, I feel an occasional twinge of apprehension when I hear a dog barking.

Extraordinary and traumatic events can scar us psychologically. Perhaps you are thinking of an event in your life that still affects you to this day. I believe that this is true concerning homosexuality.

> *Extraordinary and traumatic events can scar us psychologically.*

Not a Happy Lifestyle

Homosexual feelings are a psychological illness triggered by specific powerful and tragic events in a child's life. Three events if the child is a male, four if female. Some may be offended that I would use the term *illness* to describe homosexuality, but I do so to depict the helplessness of the injured party, not to stigmatize him or her. If someone is sick, we do not blame him; rather, we look to find out the cause of the sickness in order to apply the cure. If someone denies being sick—such as an alcoholic—there is little anyone can do to help.

This does not mean that homosexuality is not a choice; it is. But the *feelings* of same-gender preference are not a choice. I think the initial step for homosexuals is to admit their illness and not to cover it up and pretend they are not sick, or, worse, flaunt their disorder.

The American Psychiatric Association considered homosexuality to be a mental disorder until 1973 but changed its view after being pressured by gay lobbyists. The organization now claims to have come to its new conclusion from consulting with professionals and experts in the field, but it is clear that some of the "experts" were practicing homosexuals who convinced the APA to remove homosexuality from the list of mental disorders.[9]

I believe that through this change, the APA has done a great disservice to the wounded and hurting in the homosexual community. As a result of a desire to be politically correct, the APA is now partially responsible for the outbreak of sexually transmitted diseases—like AIDS and hepatitis B—that have taken the lives of many capable young people. Today, the average life span of a practicing male homosexual is forty-two years. If there were any other lifestyle choices that had the potential to shorten a person's life span by almost half, you would think that the medical community would be screaming

[9]Dr. Ronald Bayer, a pro-homosexual psychiatrist, described this event in his book *Homosexuality and American Psychiatry* (Princeton, NJ: Princeton University Press, 1981).

in order to draw attention to these poor choices. They have done so with smoking, sugar and salt consumption, and overeating, but, at most, these vices reduce a person's life span by only a few years. Yet, the medical community remains mostly silent about homosexual activity because it is not politically correct to criticize this lifestyle choice or to label it as the disease it is. It is not the job of the medical community to be politically correct. Its members need to be blunt and tell the truth, no matter how it may offend people.

> *It is not the job of the medical community to be politically correct. Its members need to be blunt and tell the truth, no matter how it may offend people.*

Since they don't want to tell the truth about this lifestyle choice, I will. Here are the awful facts about homosexuality. Seventy-three percent of psychiatrists admit that homosexuals are less happy than the average person—70 percent of them say that their unhappiness is *not* due to social stigmatization.[10]

In various studies, researchers have found that depression strikes homosexual youth four to five times more severely than their straight peers. According to the U.S. Department of Health and Human Services, gay and lesbian

[10]H. Lief, Sexual Survey Number 4: "Current Thinking on Homosexuality," *Medical Aspects of Human Sexuality* (1977): 110–11.

youth are two to three times more likely to commit suicide than other youths, and 30 percent of all youth suicides are related to the issue of sexual identity. Additionally, the rate of alcoholism is high among homosexuals. It is believed that 25 to 30 percent of homosexuals are alcoholics.[11]

One of the most disturbing statistics is that one-third of all child molestation cases involve homosexuals. This is alarming, considering that only 4 percent of the population consider themselves to be homosexual.[12] Why is the rate so much higher among homosexuals than heterosexuals? Homosexual activists love to point out that more molestation cases are committed by heterosexuals—perhaps because nearly 96 percent of the population is heterosexual—but they dismiss the fact that homosexuals are more likely than heterosexuals to be pedophiles.

Four Causes

If you are homosexual, I want to help you to understand how you became who you are—and how you can free yourself from such feelings. I have ministered to people who were hurting just like you. They wanted to be more like Jesus but struggled to overcome. Let me offer a helping

---

[11]R. Kus, "Alcoholics Anonymous and Gay America," *Medical Journal of Homosexuality*, 14, no. 2 (1987): 254.
[12]P. Cameron and others, "Child Molestation and Homosexuality," *Psychological Reports* 58 (1986): 327–37.

hand. Let me show you how to find total freedom in Christ.

The causes of homosexuality have not been a mystery. There are four unfortunate events in a child's life that can lead to a homosexual orientation.[13]

1. Sexual Abuse from an Older Person of the Same Gender

Most child molesters were themselves victims of child molestation. When a child is molested by an adult, it greatly injures that child's psyche. While many of those who have been molested never become molesters, many do develop a strange attraction to older people of the same gender. Somehow, the tragic event in their childhood caused a distortion in their minds. They associate sexual behavior with their experience and fail to realize that their same-gender attraction would not have occurred if they had not been the victims of sexual abuse.

Three-time Grammy Award winner Donnie McClurkin was raped by his uncle when he was only eight years old. Before he had ever experienced his first kiss or gone on his first date, a seed had been planted in his mind. A year later, he began to have homosexual feelings, which caused him to withdraw and act shy. On top of

---

[13]The human psyche is so complex that I do not claim that every homosexual fits neatly in one of the four categories.

this, he was raised by a sea of women. Hanging around them made him develop feminine characteristics, which didn't help his need to become a man.

He finally escaped his homosexual feelings by getting involved in music and the church. Unfortunately, he could not escape his cousin—his uncle's son—who raped him, as well. By the time Donnie was thirteen, he had been sexually abused by two older men. His effeminate disposition attracted other predatory men, who took advantage of him sexually before he was old enough to legally consent.

Donnie knew what had been done to him was wrong, but he also recognized the source of his gay feelings. He knew that he had not been made that way by God. Sinful men had made him that way. Sin was the cause of his so-called "orientation." Donnie read the Scripture that says there is *a time to hate* (Ecclesiastes 3:8). He had to hate what God hated. He knew he had to hate homosexuality.

I think that the first step to healing is to hate what God hates. Donnie hated homosexuality so much that he worked hard to overcome it. He immersed himself in the Word. His uncle had planted the seed of sexual confusion in his mind, and Donnie needed God to plant a seed of his identity in Christ in his heart. He learned that his attraction to members of the same gender was a lie that obscured his real identity in Chris. Therefore, he constantly confessed who he was in Christ. Today, Donnie McClurkin maintains that the homosexual feelings he had when he was young are no longer there.

Today, there are many Donnie McClurkins in the church who admit that they were sexually molested as children. Is it a coincidence that they are confused about their identity? Don't buy the lie that you were born that way or made that way by God. Be honest. The sins of others have bruised you so badly that you have become confused.

2. Neglect by a Parent of the Same Gender

We often hear stories of men who are attracted to older male homosexuals in a subconscious attempt to gain the love their fathers never gave them. To know the love of one's parents is a universal need, and when someone is deprived of parental love from Mom or Dad, harmful results often ensue. For example, a girl who does not feel loved by her father will often be attracted to other father figures. This also occurs with sons who lack the love of their fathers. They tend to turn toward older men. What they seek is genuine love, but what they get is often a

> *When someone is deprived of parental love from Mom or Dad, harmful results often ensue.*

sexual relationship that they mistake for genuine love. It is damaging and hurtful, but it is the only love they know.

3. A Sense of Being Out of Place with Peers of the Same Gender

It is essential that every child feel accepted by his or her same-gender peers. If a boy grows up feeling out of place and nervous around other boys, he may begin to equate such feelings of anxiety with his sensual, post pubescent feelings—those first-time experiences of sexual tension.

David was a boy who fit numerous profiles we've mentioned. His father neglected him, and he felt out of place among his same-gender peers. He and his twin brother were the youngest sons of five children. David's father favored his brother, while his mother favored him. He attended a small Baptist church, accepted Christ, and was baptized by age eleven. Eventually, he grew bored of the church because it seemed that all he heard people there talk about was salvation.

At school, he had trouble connecting with other boys. He was not especially masculine, and the other boys made fun of him. He drifted away from them and developed a better rapport with girls.

He confesses, "My longing for acceptance now turned sexual." In college, he met a popular boy who shared his homosexual longings. They engaged in sex, but David felt disgusted afterward.

After graduation, David moved to Nashville and went into the music business. He became active in computer chat rooms, at first to participate in discussions about music. Eventually, however, to connect with other homosexual men in the industry, he started frequenting Internet chat rooms. David experimented in cybersex with some of the men in these chat rooms, which began his downward spiral into a homosexual lifestyle that almost ruined his relationship with God.

In time, David grew tired of the life he was leading. He was not ready to give in to the gay philosophy that tried to force him to embrace his sexual orientation. He searched online to find other Christians who were struggling with homosexuality and eventually found the organization Exodus International. Through their help and guidance, he found a church that mixed love with fear. The congregation refused to accept homosexuality as a viable lifestyle but was compassionate toward people struggling with sin and offered to help him by providing accountability. Today, David is on the road to full recovery.

4. Women Who Are Hurt by Men

Charlene E. Cothran founded *Venus*, a magazine aimed at the gay community. She used her platform as a publisher to fight for the rights of gays and lesbians. Then, one day, she had an encounter with Christ and completely surrendered herself to His ways. Even though she had always known that same-sex relationships were wrong, she had simply glossed over the clear teachings of the Bible. She had made excuses for her own lesbian lifestyle. As she looked back, Charlene recognized the seed the enemy had planted in her mind.

Earlier, before her walk with Christ, she had been mistreated by several men who seemed interested only in sex. She grew disgusted with their carnal approach and eventually found women to be refreshingly different. Unlike those men, they seemed interested in her as a person, and that was attractive to her. This attraction, however, proved to be deceptive. She had allowed a few bad men in her life to ruin and distort her view of sex.

Eventually, Charlene could no longer live the way she was living. She repented.

In her own "coming out," she wrote to her readers,

Over the past 29 years of my life I have been an aggressive, creative, and strategic supporter of gay and lesbian issues. I've organized and participated in countless marches and various lobbying efforts in the fight for equal treatment of gay men and lesbians. I have kept current on the issues and made financial contributions to those organizations doing work about which I was most passionate. As the publisher of a 13-year-old periodical which targets Black gays and lesbians, I have had the opportunity to publicly address thousands, influencing closeted people to "come out" and stand up for themselves, which is particularly difficult in the African-American community. But now, I must come out of the closet again. I have recently experienced the power of change that came over me once I completely surrendered to the teachings of Jesus Christ. As a believer of the word of God, I fully accept and have always known that same-sex relationships are not what God intended for us.[14]

You can try to find Scriptures to justify homosexuality, but the Word of God will continue to speak the truth. God did not make anyone to be a homosexual. Once you accept this, you are on your way to change.

---

[14]Charlene E. Cothran, "Redeemed! 10 Ways to Get Out of the Gay Life, If You Want Out," *Venus* (October 2006).

Chapter Fifteen

God's Cure for Homosexuality

If you are struggling with same-sex feelings, be honest with yourself. Perhaps one of the tragic events described in the previous chapter—or something similar—has caused these feelings in your soul. Don't discount the root of your homosexual desire. To do so only postpones or completely cancels the healing you need.

It is important to understand the cause of your gay feelings, for when you discover the truth—and open yourself to the truth—you can experience the healing that Christ offers. Jesus is truth, but to deny the truth or to discount its importance is to keep the Lord from healing you.

Those who try to hide the painful events responsible for their homosexual feelings

> *Jesus is truth, but to deny the truth or to discount its importance is to keep the Lord from healing you.*

actually give power to the people who abused, neglected, molested, or otherwise hurt them. Whether you conceal your gay urges or convince yourself that they're normal, either way, you give power to the person or people who hurt you.

There is a great sense of strength that comes when you defeat a psychological weakness that was caused in part by others.

On the other hand, healing and deliverance will give you power over those who have hurt you. There is a great sense of strength that comes when you defeat a psychological weakness that was caused in part by others. There is no authority in your life if you succumb to the emotional pains brought on by the bad behavior of others. In other words, a homosexual who works at overcoming his or her same-sex feelings is actually working against those who have wounded him or her. That is power!

At this point, someone might say, "Well, even if the causes you mentioned are true, my psyche is so damaged that it is pointless to try to change. I will only be disappointed when I don't change, and then I will experience even more rejection."

This argument is an excuse to remain psychologically ill. I don't see how that is love. Love seeks to heal. My ministry is built on healing the whole person, and I am sure the Lord can heal the damaged psyches of homosexuals.

People will challenge me to leave the homosexuals alone, but I cannot allow people to remain sick when I know the cure.

The real trouble with those in the medical field is doubt. They do not believe in the supernatural power of God. They are left with their own abilities, and they find that they are not capable of bringing change to the homosexual. What I find troubling about the professionals is their criticism of the healing ministry of the church. Whether they know it or not, they are criticizing the church for believing in the divine power of God to heal and change.

If these so-called experts had been lived during the time of the early church period, they would have censured Paul for writing,

> *Neither the sexually immoral nor idolaters nor adulterers nor male prostitutes nor homosexual offenders nor thieves nor the greedy nor drunkards nor slanderers nor swindlers will inherit the kingdom of God. And that is what some of you were. But you were washed, you were sanctified, you were justified in the name of the Lord Jesus Christ and by the Spirit of our God.*
> (1 Corinthians 6:9–11)

Notice that Paul said that some of the converts were once *"homosexual offenders."* Then, he said, *"That is what some of you were."* It seems that they had changed. They were not homosexuals anymore; God had touched them, and His touch had healed them. Paul mentioned three things here that made the transformation.

1. They were washed.

But you were washed....

(1 Corinthians 6:11)

We all are dirty when we come to Christ. No one is without sin.

We all are dirty when we come to Christ. No one is without sin. We all needed cleansing from our filth, whether we were adulterers, thieves, or homosexuals. The washing comes in two ways: the new birth (see John 3:3, 7) and the washing of water through the Word. (See Ephesians 5:26.)

Something miraculous takes place when we are born again. Words cannot explain all that happens. I have heard numerous testimonies from people who struggled with homosexual feelings but were miraculously changed into heterosexuals after they were saved. Let's face it: without the new birth, a homosexual is unlikely to change. He must be born again, a process by which God cleanses the sinner and makes him new.

Concerning the new birth, Jesus said, *"I tell you the truth, no one can enter the kingdom of*

God unless he is born of water and the Spirit" (John 3:5). There are two aspects of the new birth: first, the invisible power of the Spirit, and second, the visible water of baptism. When a person sincerely calls on the Lord for salvation, the Spirit performs a numinous work in the heart of the individual. The person must also be baptized in water.

At this point, someone might say, "But, pastor, I still have those homosexual tendencies, so how can I be baptized unless God changes me? I will feel like a hypocrite if I am baptized."

Paul insisted that a person is changed by being *"washed."* It is through baptism itself that God can perform a special work—the work of cleansing. Let the Lord cleanse you from your sins. A person who waits to be baptized until after he feels clean has it in reverse. You don't wait until you feel clean to take a bath; you take a bath to become clean.

The same is true of baptism. You do not wait to feel totally clean and changed before being baptized; you let the water of baptism cleanse you. God will use that simple act of baptism to bring a miraculous change in you.

You might wonder if I would baptize someone who was still

> *You do not wait to feel totally clean and changed before being baptized; you let the water of baptism cleanse you.*

struggling with homosexual feelings. Of course I would; that is what salvation is about. I don't wait for people to change first before bringing them to Christ. No, I bring them to Christ so that He can change them.

The other way to become cleansed is through the Word of God. Jesus said, *"You are already clean because of the word I have spoken to you"* (John 15:3). The Word of God is all-powerful. Man's words have only limited power. They can't accomplish the impossible—only God can. When God speaks into the soul of man, a miracle takes place. As the homosexual takes the message of Christ into his heart, a phenomenon occurs—he finds that he is pruned like a bush. This pruning may hurt at first, but then, he finds that he becomes more fruitful for Christ. This process is a gradual one, as my next point brings out.

2. They were sanctified.

...you were sanctified....

(1 Corinthians 6:11)

To be sanctified is to be separate from the world in order to be brought near to Christ. This is an ongoing process. None of us can say that right after we were born again, we were completely the way we should be. Hopefully, we are constantly changing to be more like the Lord, but none of us has arrived.

Do not be discouraged if you do not find complete change the moment you are born again. But as you allow the Word, the Spirit, the blood of Jesus, and the activities and work of the church into your life, you will find that the influence of the world has less

> *Do not be discouraged if you do not find complete change the moment you are born again.*

and less power over you. But that won't happen if you stay away from the church.

Because of the deep nature of their hurt, homosexuals may need to be healed from the scars of their pasts. If that is your situation, you need to open yourself to someone skilled and knowledgeable in the Word. Confess your weaknesses. Share your struggle. You will be able to receive deep, personal ministry by a loving pastor who will show you supernaturally how the abuse, neglect, or rejection of your past generated within you the same-sex feelings you experience. Only by forgiving others—the abuser, the negligent parent, or the teasing peers—can you release your pain. There will be no healing unless you forgive those who wronged you.

If you were abused as a child, you must forgive the person responsible, although it may be the hardest thing you have ever done. This person might be a relative or even a religious leader, but you must release him and completely forgive him. As you forgive that person, you are releasing yourself from the power he has had over your life.

You may need to forgive a negligent father. He may have abandoned you. He may not have been there when you needed him. Yet you must still forgive. Without forgiveness, you put yourself in a prison, and that prison may include homosexual feelings.

The boys at school who teased you, who called you a "queer"—yes, you must forgive them, too. The girls who called you a tomboy—yes, you must forgive them, too. I know it's hard, but you are only allowing them to have power over your life if you do not forgive.

As you forgive, you may experience a battle. This battle is a sign that demons took advantage of you when you were young and came to oppress your life. At this point, you may need to find someone who will pray deliverance over you. But as you forgive, you will find yourself being released from these demons. They will come out of you.

3. They were justified.

...you were justified.... (1 Corinthians 6:11)

To be justified is to be totally forgiven and made right with God, as though you had never sinned. Often, someone struggling with deeply embedded sins will find it difficult to receive forgiveness. But you must!

Don't allow any disorder to deceive you into thinking that God has not forgiven you. At this point, you must resist practicing the gay lifestyle. Such practices will only hamper your complete sanctification and healing. Worse, they will bring needless judgment on you.

Paul mentioned this judgment in 1 Corinthians 11:29–30:

For anyone who eats and drinks without recognizing the body of the Lord eats and drinks judgment on himself. That is why many among you are weak and sick, and a number of you have fallen asleep.

I am convinced that many believers who have rebelled against the work of sanctification have only brought judgment on themselves. In this verse, Paul describes this judgment as weakness, sickness, and premature death.

Many homosexual Christians have become ill, and a number have died early, because they brought such self-judgment on themselves while refusing godly judgment. Godly judgment exists not for punishment, but so that they might be saved. Paul went on to write, *"When we are judged by the Lord, we are being disciplined so that we*

If you believe the lie that God has stopped loving you because you have failed Him, then the devil will take advantage of you and bring you back into a sinful lifestyle.

will not be condemned with the world" (verse 32).

God forgives you even though you have failed Him. If you believe the lie that God has stopped loving you because you have failed Him, then the devil will take advantage of you and bring you back into the sinful lifestyle. Believe in God's love for you! His love is a transforming love.

The Need for Love

The cure for homosexuality is rather simple. It is love—genuine love. Ultimately, that is what every person needs in order to change, including the homosexual.

Experiencing the real, unconditional love of God is the beginning of healing. For some, this alone brings the cure. They lose the strong feelings of same-sex attraction. Others continue to struggle with it, but as they open themselves more and more to God's love, those feelings begin to dissipate.

Finally, you must fill the need for love with the genuine platonic love of brothers and sisters in the Lord. To begin with, look no further than your pastor. Let him begin to mentor you.

Will those same-sex feelings completely leave? Perhaps not. Just as I still feel an initial tinge of fear when I hear a dog bark, you may still feel some hint of same-gender feelings, but they will no longer control you. You will begin to feel sexual attraction for the opposite gender. Over time, your feelings will begin to normalize so that you can walk with the Lord without hindrance.

For instance, my fear of dogs does not keep me from taking walks in my neighborhood. I may hear dogs barking, but the emotional scar is healed. I am no longer crippled by the incident in my childhood. It will be the same for those of you who have struggled with same-gender feelings. Your scar will be healed. The past will no longer cripple your walk with God. You will find yourself rejoicing as you experience the liberty that Christ offers.

It is essential for you to continue to abide in the Word as God uses it to heal your remaining scars.

Eventually, the Word of God will cleanse your mind from any negative, ungodly feelings. Thus, it is essential for you to continue to abide in the Word as God uses it to heal your remaining scars.

The Road to Recovery

The pursuit of holiness is a road. Driving down that road is a process; don't be discouraged if you have not yet arrived.

And a highway will be there; it will be called the Way of Holiness. The unclean will not journey on it; it will be for those who walk in that Way; wicked fools will not go about on it. (Isaiah 35:8)

Holiness is like walking on the highway. It is dangerous, there is a risk, but those who wish to be clean will take that road. The *"wicked fools"*—those who pretend to be right—will not even try to walk that road. I encourage you to walk the *"Way of Holiness."*

No lion will be there, nor will any ferocious beast get up on it; they will not be found there. But only the redeemed will walk there. (verse 9)

God will protect you from temptation. The devil will not be strong enough to drag you from that road.

They will enter Zion with singing; everlasting joy will crown their heads. Gladness and joy will overtake them, and sorrow and sighing will flee away. (verse 10)

In the end, you will rejoice in your complete victory! Eventually, the harmful feelings of homosexuality will flee. Total change, however, does not usually come all at once.

Repentance, Repair, and Restoration

There are three phases of change: repentance, repair, and restoration. Restoration is that final and glorious change God makes in us in which sin is no longer pressing against us. We are restored to a complete wholeness in body and mind. But we cannot arrive at that final stage until we come through the first two stages: repentance and repair.

> *You cannot wait for the feelings to change before you change. Everyone has the power to say no to sin.*

Many want to repent only when they no longer experience temptation. Someone might say, "When God removes my homosexual feelings, then I will stop practicing homosexuality." This is the wrong order. You cannot wait for the feelings to change before you change. Everyone has the power to say no to sin.

> *For the grace of God that brings salvation has appeared to all men. It teaches us to say "No" to ungodliness and worldly passions, and to live self-controlled, upright and godly lives in this present age.*
>
> (Titus 2:11–12)

You do not stop being ungodly by waiting until your *"worldly passions"* are gone. You say no, even though the worldly passions are still present. This is obvious to us when it comes to most sins, but people fool themselves when it comes to homosexuality. They march for their rights to be able to say yes to ungodliness. You do not find adulterers marching for their right to cheat on their wives. You don't find thieves marching for their right to steal. There are lots of things we may want, but we learn to say no.

Even if you still carry the feelings of same-sex attraction, that does not make you a homosexual. A homosexual is not one by *orientation* but by *action*. A thief who stops stealing is no longer a thief. He may still want something that belongs to someone else, but if he does not take it, he is not a thief. And so it is with you. If you repent, you are no longer a homosexual. Don't let the world and the devil tell you that you are a homosexual simply because you have feelings of same-sex attraction. Those feelings are lies and temptations of the devil.

One of my heroes at our church is Marcos. At one time, he was a transvestite because his male lover insisted that he dress up like a woman. Eventually, to please this man, he began the process of a sex change. He was only a couple of days away from the final operation when it hit him: he was doing all this for one man. He decided not to go through with it, and his relationship with the other man ended.

Marcos returned to his mother's church, and there, God began to perform an incredible miracle in his life. He repented of his sin, got rid of his breast implants, and has been walking with the Lord ever since. Today, Marcos is living a life of holiness, and he sings with the worship team at our church. He admits that he still finds men attractive, but he refuses to act on those feelings. To me, this is the greatest sign of holiness. It is easy to walk the road of holiness when you feel like it. It is harder to do the right thing when you feel like doing the wrong thing. I believe that Marcos will eventually receive a total transformation of his feelings, but in the meantime, he is walking the road of holiness. As he is doing, you must walk the road of holiness.

As you walk the road of holiness, you will find God coming to repair your damaged psyche. It may come in the form of a timely word from God, a special gift of the Spirit, or a power encounter in the middle of the night. It may even take the form of deliverance.

Maria was an avowed lesbian. Her mother was also a lesbian, and Maria remembers sleeping naked between her mother and her lover at the age of three. Although no sexual contact took place, she remembers feeling that the situation was wrong. She believes that an evil spirit came into her life at that moment.

At the age of nine, Maria experienced her first feelings of attraction toward a female nurse and accepted the fact that she was a lesbian. Interestingly, she also felt attracted to men, but she quickly dismissed this as a false feeling. Instead, she gave herself over to a lesbian lifestyle.

Ironically, at the age of twenty-six, she met her future husband at a strip club. They eventually married, and both of them came to the Lord. Despite coming to Christ, however, Maria still felt bound by lesbianism. Occasionally, she continued in this practice. Her husband was forgiving, but she needed something more than salvation. Then, she heard about deliverance.

At a seminar about spiritual warfare, Maria came forward for prayer. As the minister commanded the demon of homosexuality to come out, Maria felt the evil spirit struggle within her and eventually be expelled. Maria claims that she immediately lost any sexual desire for women. Since that day, she has never acted on lesbian feelings.

I believe that some people need a dramatic deliverance like this. If you think you need deliverance, seek a Bible-based minister who believes in it and get him or her to pray for you. This will be an important step toward repairing your emotions. However, it is just one of many steps God offers to repair your life. And through God's process, you will find your mind being repaired as a total restoration takes place.

Part III

Spiritual Diseases

Chapter Sixteen

Can the Human Spirit Become Sick?

There is much controversy over the topic of the human spirit, especially regarding the issue of whether the born-again human spirit can become sick. Opinions are subjective. Thankfully, the Word of God answers the question.

Some people ask whether humans even *have* a spirit. Some see mankind as consisting of only mind and body. We do have a spirit, however, which helps to explain why humans are the only creatures on earth who are religious. Religion is a uniquely human institution.

Anthropologists have developed theories about the evolution of religion. Some speculate that the desire for immortality is the seed of religion. However, that does not answer the question of why we desire immortality. Some say mankind fears the unseen, so he dreams up theories about God, angels, and demons. Again, this does not explain why mankind believes in the unseen, while animals do not. Critics of the creation account in Scripture admit that humans have the highest intelligence of all the earth's creatures, yet these same critics put themselves in a quandary when they dismiss the notion that man has a spirit made in the image of God. Even the most skeptical critic must admit that mankind is uniquely different from the animals because of two things: man has a soul and a spirit.

Biological, Psychological, and Spiritual Needs

Mankind's primary needs are threefold, springing from his three main components: body, soul, and spirit. Or, to use more technical terminology, mankind's needs are biological, psychological, and spiritual. Consider the three most basic physical needs of all creatures, whether human or animal: eating, sleeping, and sex. Unlike animals, whose physical needs are met by these three things, humans benefit from them psychologically and spiritually, as well as physically.

Animals eat when they are hungry. Humans, however, will eat for social reasons, as well as to satisfy hunger. We have developed human rituals around food. We are the only creatures who cook and season our food. We do not simply take food and put it into our mouths. No! We cook it, put it on plates, and eat it with utensils, and we share this routine with other people. Why? Because there is more at stake than just satisfying our physical needs. There is also a psychological component. Eating can also meet our spiritual needs. For example, at the dinner table, we may bow our heads and gives thanks to God by praying over our food. Animals do not do that.

Some faith traditions take this even further by letting food represent divinity. Some believe that in taking Communion, we are partaking of divinity. As you can see, humans eat to serve not just their biological needs but their psychological and spiritual needs, as well.

The same can be said of sleep. Animals sleep whenever they are tired. Humans schedule their sleep times. We do not simply lie down wherever we can; we make a bed and put covers on it. We may put on specific clothes for sleeping. This ritual is clearly different from that of animals. Sleep can even be spiritual. While humans and animals both dream in their sleep, humans sometimes see their dreams as possible words from God—omens or warnings about the future. For humans, dreaming can be a spiritual event.

Sex is another area in which humans differ from animals. One obvious difference is that animals do not cover their procreative parts with clothing. Humans do. Humans are also the only ones who make love face-to-face. This is to meet a psychological need. Animals will freely have sex in public. They do it when they want to, without a care for who is watching. Humans retreat into private quarters and close the door. (Unfortunately, pornographers have turned sex into a public, animalistic act, but this is not the norm.) For humans, sex can also be a spiritual act when a husband and wife consummate their lifetime commitment. Animals, of course, do not marry. Humans, especially Christians, marry not only for psychological reasons, but also for spiritual ones. They acknowledge that when two people are married, God has joined them in holy matrimony.

As you can tell, man is more than mind and body; he is also a spirit made in God's image.

What Is the Spirit?

The human spirit is the "umbilical cord" that connects us to God. It makes us aware of God's existence. It is our "God side." It is what makes us most like God. Godliness is the product of the human spirit. Any good we do comes from the human spirit. Unfortunately, the evil we do can also proceed from an unregenerate spirit. As Jesus said, *"The good man brings good things out of the good stored up*

> *Godliness is the product of the human spirit. Any good we do comes from the human spirit.*

in him, and the evil man brings evil things out of the evil stored up in him" (Matthew 12:35).

The human spirit gives us our conscious awareness of eternity. *"[God] has also set eternity in the hearts of men"* (Ecclesiastes 3:11). Nearly every religion believes in life after death. This belief comes from the awareness of God that exists in the human spirit.

The human spirit can also help us to connect with the unseen, demonic spiritual world. Supernatural phenomena, such as out-of-body experiences, contacting the dead, and forecasting the future, are all deceptions of the devil within the human spirit. Such "spiritists" claim to use their spirits to contact other human spirits. Unfortunately, many are unaware that they are not contacting human spirits but demonic ones. Because of this, the Bible forbids such practices. Of the dead, God says, *"They are now dead, they live no more; those departed spirits do not rise"* (Isaiah 26:14). In other words, departed spirits cannot contact the living, and the living cannot contact them.

Intuitive feelings, though not logical, are fruits of the human spirit. We may feel that something is about to happen, but we have no tangible proof. We call it a "gut feeling."

According to Scripture, man's spirit—not his soul—also contains his motives. The Bible says that God *"will expose the motives of men's hearts"* (1 Corinthians 4:5). The conscience is the voice of God speaking to the human spirit. Though we may try to rationalize our behavior, God's voice will always speak to our spirits, loud and clear.

A Contaminated Spirit

No Christian minister doubts the depravity of the human spirit. The human spirit is capable of all kinds of atrocities. As one of the prophets said, *"The heart is deceitful above all things and beyond cure"* (Jeremiah 17:9). If the human heart is *"beyond cure,"* that means there must be a sickness involved. But what of the born-again spirit? Can a regenerate human spirit become sick?

> *Since we have these promises, dear friends, let us purify ourselves from everything that contaminates body and spirit, perfecting holiness out of reverence for God.*
>
> (2 Corinthians 7:1)

Here, the apostle Paul was writing to believers, urging them to purify themselves *"from everything that contaminates body and spirit."* No one will disagree that man's body can become physically contaminated. If that's the case, why can't the same thing happen to the spirit? Paul would not have encouraged the cleansing of the human spirit if it did not need to be cleansed. You cleanse something only if it gets dirty. The

human spirit can get dirty, contaminated, and sick.

The human spirit can get dirty, contaminated, and sick.

Remember what Paul said about the threefold nature of man: *"May your whole spirit, soul and body be kept blameless at the coming of our Lord Jesus Christ"* (1 Thessalonians 5:23). This benediction suggests that the spirit needs God's power to *"be kept blameless."* Theologians do not question whether the body or soul can become sick, yet this passage teaches that the human spirit also needs God's sanctifying work.

I believe that the worst type of sickness is a spiritual sickness. God's Word says, *"A man's spirit sustains him in sickness"* (Proverbs 18:14). Even in sickness, a man's spirit may be able to sustain him, perhaps giving him the strength to recover. But what happens when the human spirit becomes sick? Then, there is nothing left to sustain him. A man's body can't heal his spirit. A man's soul cannot heal his spirit. When a man's spirit is sick, he has little hope of recovery. Thankfully, God is willing and able to forgive you and to set you free from the power that Satan has over your life. But the first step in being set free is to understand our enemy.

Chapter Seventeen

The World of the Occult

Somewhere in nearly all of us is a desire to contact the unknown—a higher power that is greater, wiser, and more powerful than we are. This type of curiosity can lead people to delve into the occult. The word *occult* comes from a Latin word meaning "concealed or covered over, secret." It is knowledge of the supernatural.

There is nothing intrinsically wrong with supernatural knowledge. God often imparts supernatural knowledge to those who seek it. The real issue is the source of that supernatural knowledge. Is it coming from God, or from some other supernatural being?

God created both a natural and a spiritual world. The natural world is a tangible realm that can be seen and studied through fact. The spiritual world is an unseen realm that can be understood properly through God alone. Science can explain the first world. Religion attempts to explain the second. Religion depends on the conscience. The word *conscience* comes from two words: *con*, meaning "with," and *science*, meaning "knowledge or a system of knowledge covering general truths or the operation of general laws." Science deals with math, astronomy, chemistry, literature, and all the other physical arts and sciences. Conscience deals with questions that science cannot answer. Religion is *divine* science, and it should work alongside *natural* science. Neither should compete with the other. Science can't answer religious questions, and religion was not meant to answer specific scientific questions. Science has its limitations.

> *Religion is divine science, and it should work alongside natural science. Neither should compete with the other.*

Although scientists study many objects and events, there are things they cannot test. A scientist cannot measure a mother's love for her children. He cannot measure the difference between good and evil.[15]

For example, science can tell you what Adolf Hitler did during the Holocaust, but it can't answer whether or not he was "evil." Questions of good and evil are not for science to answer.

[15] *World Book Encyclopedia*, 1976, Volume 14, s.v. "Occult," p. 64.

Science deals with observable and measurable facts, not the spiritual realm. Questions of good and evil are for the conscience. Science is, therefore, limited to the natural world. It is left to religion to answer questions about the spiritual world.

What Is True Religion?

There are basically three religious views:

• Polytheism—the belief in many gods.

• Pantheism—the belief that god is in the elements.

• Monotheism—the belief in one God.

Polytheism was the predominant worldview before Christianity. In those days, people believed that certain natural elements—the wind, the sun, the moon, and so forth—were spirit beings. They worshipped these things as gods. This was the practice of the citizens of Greece and Rome. It was the practice of the Native Americans. And, it is still practiced today in parts of the world. In India, for example, Hinduism is widespread; it is the largest polytheistic religion on earth. Yoga has become a popular activity in the West, but it is a product of Hinduism. Concepts such as reincarnation and karma are Hindu ideas.

Pantheism is the belief that God and the universe are one and the same thing, and that God does not exist as a separate spirit. Witches—or

Wiccans—are often pantheistic in their beliefs. They view objects as having a divine force that can be used to channel God's energy.

The predominant worldview today is monotheism—the belief that one God created and reigns over the entire universe, much like a builder reigns over the structure he is building. The builder is not in the bricks or cement he uses on the building; he exists separately from them.

The three major world religions are monotheistic: Christianity, Judaism, and Islam. Each of these religions expresses concern over man's attempt to delve into the spiritual world without God's approval.

Spiritual Deception

The Hebrew Scriptures specifically warn against delving into the spiritual world outside of God's direction.

When you enter the land the Lord your God is giving you, do not learn to imitate the detestable ways of the nations there. Let no one be found among you who sacrifices his son or daughter in the fire, who practices divination or sorcery, interprets omens, engages in witchcraft, or casts spells, or who is a medium or spiritist or who consults the dead. Anyone who does these things is detestable to the Lord, and because of these detestable practices the LORD *your God will drive out those nations before you. You must be blameless before the Lord your God.* (Deuteronomy 18:9–13)

God has placed a longing within us to know the realm of the Spirit, but His archenemy, Satan, has invented ways to divert people into deceptive, evil systems that bring them into bondage to himself. These deceptive systems can take countless different forms, but the standard name for all of them is the occult. In ancient Israel, they took such forms as divination, sorcery, witchcraft, casting spells, and consulting the dead. Even though many of these things are found on Main Street, USA, they have been around for thousands of years.

Movies, television shows, and video games work at making the occult seem harmless, attractive, and even fun. But make no mistake: the occult is harmful. If it were so harmless, then why would God have given us such clear warnings to avoid it?

Is It Really Wrong?

The world—including Christians—has become desensitized to the occult. Consider this stern warning about participation in the occult:

The acts of the sinful nature are obvious: sexual immorality, impurity and debauchery; idolatry and witchcraft; hatred, discord, jealousy, fits of rage, selfish ambition, dissensions, factions and envy; drunkenness, orgies, and the like. I warn you, as I did before, that those who live like this will not inherit the kingdom of God. (Galatians 5:19–21)

Look at the list carefully. The *"acts of the sinful nature"* are grouped into four categories, which are divided by semicolons. The first group includes sexual sins, the second group includes occult sins, the third group includes hate sins, and the fourth group includes licentious sins. Some of these may be problem areas for you, while others may not be. However, according to the Word, they all are sins.

Politicians often argue over these activities. Liberals tend to lobby against hate sins, such as racism and discrimination, while Conservatives tend to lobby against sexual sins, such as pornography. In truth, we should be against all forms of sin. We should not group them in order of seriousness. Sin is wrong, period! God does not give us the option to declare what is right or wrong. He alone declares what is right and wrong; our

> *God does not give us the option to declare what is right or wrong. He alone declares what is right and wrong; our only choice is to agree or rebel.*

only choice is to agree or rebel. I've decided not to allow the current culture to influence me by telling me what is right and wrong. For me, God is the judge—no one else—and He has judged all categories of sin as being evil.

One of those categories is the occult. Paul condemned two forms of the occult: idolatry and witchcraft. Idolatry is related to polytheism while witchcraft is related to pantheism. So, Paul condemns both polytheism and pantheism in his first letter to the Corinthians: *"The sacrifices of pagans are offered to demons, not to God, and I do not want you to be participants with demons"* (verse 10:20). This is a reference to the practice of offering sacrifices to idols. Both of these religions use deceptive methods to delve into the unknown realm of the spirit, or in an attempt to make contact with a supernatural god or gods. When people try to tap into the spiritual world in an unauthorized manner, they expose themselves to demons.

An example of deliverance from occult spirits was recorded by Luke in the book of Acts.

Once when we were going to the place of prayer, we were met by a slave girl who had a spirit by which she predicted the future. She earned a great deal of money for her owners by fortune-telling. This girl followed Paul and the rest of us, shouting, "These men are servants of the Most

High God, who are telling you the way to be saved." She kept this up for many days. Finally Paul became so troubled that he turned around and said to the spirit, "In the name of Jesus Christ I command you to come out of her!" At that moment the spirit left her. When the owners of the slave girl realized that their hope of making money was gone, they seized Paul and Silas and dragged them into the marketplace to face the authorities. (Acts 16:16–19)

This young girl had a rare ability to predict the future. According to this passage, *"a spirit"* gave her this ability, and when Paul drove the spirit out, she lost this power. With this power, she had made her owners a lot of money. There is money to be made in the occult. One need only look at the proliferation of psychic hotlines as evidence of this.

Interestingly, this girl appears to have advocated for Christianity. She shouted, *"These men are servants of the Most High God, who are telling you the way to be saved."* The thing that fools some Christians about the occult is that fortune-tellers and psychics often appear to talk about the God of the Bible. They may sound Christian, but their practice is strictly occult. Paul was not fooled by such a deceptive witness for the Lord. You shouldn't be, either.

Finally, there was a battle for the minds of the watching community. The owners of this girl had Paul and Silas arrested, beaten, and imprisoned. After God sent an earthquake to break open their jail cell, the city authorities ordered them to leave the city. (See Acts 16:25–39.)

There is still a battle raging over our communities. I notice how hard the occult community can be on Christians, as fortune-tellers and others who dabble in the occult fight to preserve the incomes they receive from these practices. The advantage some occultists have against us is money, which they will use to promote their practices in the media. But, as Paul demonstrated, the power of the Holy Spirit is greater than the power of Satan.

Witchcraft

He sacrificed his sons in the fire in the Valley of Ben Hinnom, practiced sorcery, divination and witchcraft, and consulted mediums and spiritists. He did much evil in the eyes of the Lord, provoking him to anger. (2 Chronicles 33:6)

Witchcraft is not harmless, and recently, we have seen a revival of witchcraft in America— especially among young people. Harry Potter books—and the movies they have spawned—have promoted renewed interest in magic for many of the children who have read them. Lately, movies like *The Sixth Sense* and *Ghost* have made audiences curious about contacting the dead. More recently, the TV show *Crossing Over with John Edward* brought séances into America's living rooms.

For the most part, our culture sees witchcraft as harmless fun. I will admit that only a few people actually delve into the occult as a result of viewing such programs and movies, but even one person who does so is one too many.

Whenever somebody participates in witchcraft or séances, his spirit comes in contact with demons. Those demons deceive him, and that deception is the disease. Deception causes people to grow cold toward the Lord. It opens them to other doctrines that confuse their understanding of the Bible. Eventually, they may begin to deny what is essential to salvation. They may soon lose the desire to follow Christ or to be saved. They may even believe that they are saved when, in reality, they have denied who the Lord really is.

> *Deception is ingrained in the spirit and makes people hard-hearted toward the gospel.*

You do not have to be a witch to become deceived. You need only to be around one. Deception is a contagious disease that is passed on to others who expose themselves to the occult. Have you noticed how the occult tends to target children? They are inclined to be more receptive to these things than adults. If you can deceive a child, it becomes difficult to rescue that child from Satan's deception. Deception is ingrained in the spirit and makes people hard-hearted toward the gospel.

As a preteen and teenager, I used to explore the world of the occult. I dabbled with a Ouija board, magic eight balls, tarot cards, palm reading, biorhythms, and horoscopes. They seemed innocent enough at the time. Little did I know what I was getting myself into.

One day, my cousins and I were asking questions over a Ouija board and waiting for answers. One particular question we asked was when we would die. All of a sudden, we heard a loud sound that startled us. We jumped up and, after trying to calm down, went into the kitchen, where we found a broken plate on the floor. It had fallen from the cabinet all by itself. Afterward, we all agreed to get rid of the Ouija board. I can't explain what happened. I don't know if the devil threw that plate down, or whether God did it to scare us away from dabbling in the occult. All I know is that it scared us.

There are supernatural elements found in those types of things. Sometimes, supernatural or unexplained events will occur. The important thing is to stay away from all forms of witchcraft, sorcery, divination, and other occult practices that will contaminate your spirit.

"Do not give the devil a foothold" (Ephesians 4:27). A foothold is like a small opening to a door. All an intruder needs is a small opening in order to get a foot in that door, making it harder to close him out. Likewise, that is all the devil needs to gain access to your life. The occult is that little crack in the door, just wide enough to allow Satan to come in and wreak havoc in your life. Be wise. Don't give him any ground.

Chapter Eighteen

Breaking Free from the Occult

You may have been entangled in the occult, and now you want to break free. Be encouraged! As I've stated, God will forgive you and set you free from the power that Satan has over your life. How can you be set free?

As we learned in chapter three, you must get rid of any objects associated with the occult. Consider this account in Scripture:

> *Many of those who believed now came and openly confessed their evil deeds. A number who had practiced sorcery brought their scrolls together and burned them publicly. When they calculated the value of the scrolls, the total came to fifty thousand drachmas.* (Acts 19:18–19)

In this account, the people of Ephesus did two things: first, they openly confessed their evil deeds; second, they burned their scrolls. They got rid of any association with sorcery.

You need to take whatever objects are associated with the occult and burn them or throw them away. I have heard stories of such burnings that would send a chill up your spine. Some have testified that they heard screaming as they burned their occult articles.

At the age of eighteen, I was convicted by the Word of God to get rid of my collection of comic books. As I flipped through them, I noticed many references to the occult. Some portrayed "good witches" casting spells for the "benefit" of mankind. I thought, *How horrible to attempt to show witches as being good.* I wanted nothing to do with witchcraft. So, I took my stash of comic books into the backyard, dug a hole, and began to bury them. My next-door neighbor noticed what I was doing and begged to have the books. I refused. Why should I pass on a demon to someone else? You may think that what I did was extreme, but I was simply doing what the Christians at Ephesus did.

Take inventory of your house. What articles of clothing, books, videos, and games do you have that are associated with the occult? Get rid of them. By doing so, you are closing the door on the enemy.

Ask God to forgive you, and then receive His forgiveness. Renounce any association you have had with the occult. Cancel any memberships you have with occult organizations. If you are a member of a coven, withdraw your membership. Tell them that you now stand for Christ. The word *coven*—meaning "an assembly or band...of witches"—comes from the same root word as *covenant*. If you remain in the coven, you remain in covenant with the witches. You must break every evil covenant. Although prayer support is always a good thing, it is not enough for others to renounce Satan for you. You also must renounce him yourself.

> *Although prayer support is always a good thing, it is not enough for others to renounce Satan for you. You also must renounce him yourself.*

What Is Witchcraft?

Witchcraft is defined as follows: "In general, witchcraft is sorcery, the magical manipulation of the supernormal forces through the use of spells, and the conjuring or invoking of spirits."[16]

Witchcraft attempts to manipulate supernatural forces, such as spirits. If all the spirits that inhabited this world were good spirits, there would be little problem with this. But Scripture tells us that one-third of the angels in heaven were cast out with Lucifer. (See Revelation 12:4.) If one-third of spirits are evil, what are people

---

[16]Rosemary Ellen Guiley, *The Encyclopedia of Witches, Witchcraft, and Wicca* (New York: Facts on File, 2008), 378.

conjuring or trying to manipulate? What spells are they using?

To cast a spell is to use words or objects to manipulate the natural world in order to get what one wants. A witch may use such tools as drugs, potions, charms, amulets, incantations, or various forms of music.

While witches use drugs and potions in an attempt to manipulate spirits, those spirits are actually manipulating them. To see how antagonistic witchcraft is to the gospel, read the ancient requirements for being a witch:

1. Denial of the Christian faith

2. Rebaptism into the coven

3. Swearing allegiance to the devil

4. Request of the devil to write their names in the book of death[17]

Today, witchcraft may not have the same requirements, but would you really want to be associated with a "religion" like this? Especially one that historically has been hostile toward Christianity?

For years, Satan has filled popular music with themes of the occult in an attempt to reach and control our young people. This should come as no surprise, since the Bible seems to suggest

---

[17]Josh McDowell and Don Stewart, *Handbook of Today's Religions: Understanding the Occult* (San Bernardino, CA: Here's Life Publishing, 1982), 182.

that Lucifer led the music in heaven before his rebellion and expulsion. (See Isaiah 14:11–12.)

After I became saved, I took all my forms of worldly music—including a Led Zeppelin album—and crushed them. I broke free from any influence of the occult. If you want freedom from the occult, I suggest that you follow these steps:

1. Get rid of any objects associated with the occult. Gather them all together and either bury them in a grave or burn them.

2. Renounce any involvement with the occult. If you have been involved with Ouija boards, psychics, witchcraft, sorcery, mind-reading, biorhythms, astrology, or other similar practices, cease your involvement. As you get rid of occult items, say something like the following out loud: "I am sorry, Lord, for offending You by embracing the occult. I repudiate my involvement with _____ (be specific and name the objects, people, or organizations). I rebuke all demons and give them notice that I am serving God and His Son, Jesus Christ, with all of my heart. In Jesus' name, amen."

3. Ask for God's forgiveness. He is merciful and will forgive you if you sincerely ask Him to. (See 1 John 1:9.)

4. Take a stand against the enemy. The devil will not be pleased with your decision. He

will fight you. He will try to steal your joy in the Lord. He may even try to bring trouble into your life. Know that he cannot win. Satan will flee, and you will be victorious. (See James 4:7.)

Chapter Nineteen

The Trap of Satan

Diseases of the spirit affect your relationship with God. You may be sick in body and still have a great relationship with the Lord. You may even have emotional illnesses and still be able to serve God. But when your spirit is sick, your relationship with God suffers.

I have discovered a widespread spiritual disease that has become an epidemic in the body of Christ. This diabolical sickness is contagious and even life threatening, at least as far as it concerns the spiritual life of God's saints. What is this diabolical disease?

Don't have anything to do with foolish and stupid arguments, because you know they produce quarrels. And the Lord's servant must not quarrel; instead, he must be kind to everyone, able to teach, not resentful. Those who oppose him he must gently instruct, in the hope that God will grant them repentance leading them to a knowl-edge of the truth, and that they will come to their senses and escape from the trap of the devil, who has taken them captive to do his will. (2 Timothy 2:23–26)

In this passage, the apostle Paul offered a bleak picture of recovery. He hoped that *"those who op-pose* [the Lord's servant]*"* would repent and come to their senses. He *hoped* it would happen, but one gets the sense that he did not *believe* that it would. Paul talked about a "trap"—like that of a hostage who has been taken captive. Police know that when someone is abducted, the more time that goes by, the less likely his eventual recovery becomes. When hostages are released, we get excited because we are far too accustomed to hearing that the worst has occurred. The same is true with Satan's traps. They are difficult to escape.

According to Greek mythology, Ares was the Greek god of war, a strong and fierce fighter who delighted in bloody conflict. He did not simply fight to preserve his nation; he took great de-light in fighting. It was his way of life. It was more enjoyable than a friendly conversation with others.

The trap of Satan causes people to want to argue.

Like Ares, some people delight in conflict and quarreling. But Paul cautioned, *"Don't have any-thing to do with foolish and stupid arguments."* The trap of Satan causes people to want to argue. They love to fight because there is something in them that causes them to disagree vehemently with other people.

The Lure

No one purposefully falls into a trap. He must be lured into it. Satan will bait a trap so that the unsuspecting individual falls into it.

If you have ever been fishing, you probably have a favorite type of lure. You don't use it right away. You try other lures first, but when nothing else seems to work, you resort to that special bait that few fish can resist. It probably costs more, but it's worth it.

Likewise, Satan will try everything on you. He will tempt you with illicit sex, drugs, and money. If any of these work, he may control you for a while, but most believers eventually repent of these things. When that doesn't work, he may try to hurt you with trials. Even then, most believers eventually overcome the tests of life. When nothing else seems to work on you, Satan will pull out his most trusted lure. Few people ever seem to get off this hook. This lure is mentioned in Luke 17:1: *"Then said* [Jesus] *unto the disciples, It is impossible but that offenses will come: but woe unto him, through whom they come!"* (KJV).

The Greek word for *"offenses"* is *skandalon*, originally "the name of the part of a trap to

257

which the bait is attached." In other words, it is the hook. The fishing pole is the trap; the hook is the offense.

Now, perhaps, you understand why Paul told Timothy not to be resentful. (See 2 Timothy 2:24.) In other words, don't play the same game that your opponent plays. Timothy was resentful over something that he was convinced was a scandal—hence, the word *skandalon*. The scandal may have been some action that he believed was wrong. It may have been a teaching that he believed was heretical. It does not matter what it was; he had been offended. Someone had done or said something wrong, and now, Timothy wanted to argue about it. I have rarely seen someone like this repent and come to his senses through argumentation. In most cases, he goes to his grave with his anger.

Legend has it that the way poachers catch moneys in the jungle is by placing a peanut inside a jar that is tied down. The opening is barely wide enough for the monkey's hand to enter. Once the animal grabs the peanut, it is impossible for it to remove its hand from the jar along with the peanut. When the poachers arrive, the monkey knows its life is in danger. It screams and thrashes, but it does not let go of the peanut. The poachers simply grab the monkey and the jar and throw them both into a cage. Desire to have a peanut costs the monkey its freedom.

We humans are not so bright, either. We will take offense over something someone else did and then refuse to let go of that offense. The devil approaches, but instead of letting go of the offense, we scream all the louder. We are angry. Eventually, Satan throws us into a prison of our own making.

Offenses Must Come

Again, Jesus said, *"It is impossible but that offenses will come"* (Luke 17:1 KJV). There are many things that may never come again, but offenses are not one of them. They will always come. There is no point in praying that no one will offend you, because offenses will come, anyway. The question is, what will you do when they come? Will you take the lure, or will you escape?

Not only did Jesus say that offenses will come, but He also guaranteed all of His apostles that they would be offended:

> *There is no point in praying that no one will offend you, because offenses will come, anyway. The question is, what will you do when they come?*

Then saith Jesus unto them, All ye shall be offended because of me this night: for it is written, I will smite the shepherd, and the sheep of the flock shall be scattered abroad. (Matthew 26:31 KJV)

No one was excluded. *"All ye shall be offended because of me."* Jesus offended them, because He did not follow their man-made plans.

I figure that if Jesus offended all of His followers, then surely, I am going to offend my church members. I am not alone. Pastors throughout the world have to deal with offended church members. A pastor may do nearly everything right, but there will always be people who will find something wrong with him. Jesus never sinned, yet the apostles found something wrong with Him. One denied knowing Him; another betrayed Him. They all abandoned Him in His time of need.

I have joked that if all of the members that I had ever offended over the years had stayed in my church, we would be a megachurch. I'm sure most other pastors would agree. It seems that the number one reason why people leave a church is over some offense. The pastor, his wife, or some other church member has done or said something to offend them, and now they are ready to pull out their family. They may try to convince themselves that it was something else. "I don't get fed." "The praise music is not anointed." "The children's ministry lacks facilities." But really, something is bothering them. They are hurt. They feel bruised. So, they leave. But leaving is not the cure; letting go of the offense is the cure.

The Lure Is for the Big Fish

Satan rarely uses offense on the "babes in Christ." They are too easy a prey for this special lure. He will use other methods to drag their spirits down. No, this lure of offense is saved for the "super saints."

If you've ever fished, have you noticed that it is harder to catch the *bigger* fish? I normally pull in dozens of small fish. I know there are bigger ones in the lake, but they don't ever seem to bite, or, if they do, they are often too strong to reel in.

The same is true for the lure of offense. Few newer believers fall for it. They are too excited about the Lord to get bogged down with petty things. They think the pastor is the greatest preacher ever to grace the pulpit. They think the worship music is heavenly. They think the deacons are people to be respected.

But when a saint has been in the church for a long time, things begin to change. He notices that the pastor is human and makes mistakes. The "babe in Christ" may not notice it, but the spiritual man has *discernment*. After all, God is using him to straighten out all the sins of the church. He is qualified, you know!

You are not alone if you are the spiritual man who has fallen for the lure of offense. Who else is Satan going to try to catch? He is afraid of you. You have grown in your faith. Nothing he does seems to work on you. So, he pulls out his trusted lure, and—*pow!*—you are caught. What trapped you? Perhaps you noticed some flaw in your church. Suddenly, it's all you can think about. In public, you begin to deny that you are a part of *that* church. Like Judas, you are betraying those leaders who have helped you to grow. You hurt them through gossip when you try to lure others into questioning or leaving the church.

Why have you done this? You have seen a weakness in your pastor. You have seen carnality among the members of the praise and worship team. The deacons have begun to seem more like demons. And you are much too spiritual to put up with that! Right? Forgive my sarcasm, but the truth is, you have become offended.

Consider Peter and Judas. Both were offended, but only one recovered. Peter was a trusted part of Jesus' inner circle. Judas was their treasurer. You do not place the group's finances in the hands of a nobody. You give them to someone you trust. What caused Judas to betray Christ? This passage reveals the real reason.

> *Mary took about a pint of pure nard, an expensive perfume; she poured it on Jesus' feet and wiped his feet with her hair. And the house was filled with the fragrance of the perfume. But one of his disciples, Judas Iscariot, who was later to betray*

him, objected, "Why wasn't this perfume sold and the money given to the poor? It was worth a year's wages." He did not say this because he cared about the poor but because he was a thief; as keeper of the money bag, he used to help himself to what was put into it. "Leave her alone," Jesus replied. "It was intended that she should save this perfume for the day of my burial. You will always have the poor among you, but you will not always have me."

(John 12:3–8)

Judas had several character flaws—such as greed, which led to embezzling money for himself—but Peter also had character flaws, including pride and anger. Neither was perfect. The Lord seemed to be constantly rebuking Peter. *"You of little faith"* (Matthew 14:31). *"Get behind me, Satan!"* (Matthew 16:23). *"You will disown me three times!"* (John 13:38). Never, however, do we find Jesus rebuking Judas—except for this one occasion.

Unlike Peter, Judas seemed to have a good case. Mary had poured perfume on Jesus that cost a year's wages. Be honest. Doesn't that sound wasteful? How do you feel when your pastor buys an expensive car? Does it seem like a waste of money? At least a car has some practical use, but perfume? Couldn't she have found something cheaper? But Jesus allowed it, and Judas objected.

Let's read a parallel passage about this story that will shed more light on it. Please, don't be tempted to skip over this passage. It gives us great insight into Judas's thinking.

> While [Jesus] *was in Bethany, reclining at the table in the home of a man known as Simon the Leper, a woman came with an alabaster jar of very expensive perfume, made of pure nard. She broke the jar and poured the perfume on his head. Some of those present were saying indignantly to one another, "Why this waste of perfume? It could have been sold for more than a year's wages and the money given to the poor." And they rebuked her harshly. "Leave her alone," said Jesus. "Why are you bothering her? She has done a beautiful thing to me. The poor you will always have with you, and you can help them any time you want. But you will not always have me. She did what she could. She poured perfume on my body beforehand to prepare for my burial. I tell you the truth, wherever the gospel is preached throughout the world, what she has done will also be told, in memory of her."* (Mark 14:3–9)

Did you see it? Look for Judas. He is not mentioned in this passage. Mark recorded only that *"some of those present"* rebuked Mary. We know from John's gospel that Judas led the group in their opposition of this waste of perfume. This gives an insight into what was happening. Judas was a leader, and he seemed to have the majority on his side. It is easy not to see the offense when it appears that so many others agree with you. This also is a trick of the enemy. The majority is not always right.

> *It is easy not to see the offense when it appears that many others agree with you. This also is a trick of the enemy. The majority is not always right.*

Not only did Jesus rebuke Judas, but He did so in front of the group. Jesus rebuked Peter in front of the group many times. Judas, though, was different. He was in charge of the money. His opinion mattered. Money was his specialty. If anyone should have known how the money was to be spent, it was Judas. Jesus, however, did not seem impressed with Judas's credentials.

Jesus not only rebuked Judas in front of his peers, but He also added, *"I tell you the truth, wherever the gospel is preached throughout the world, what she has done will also be told, in memory of her"* (Mark 14:9). This incident would not be kept secret. The whole world would know what Judas had done. That hurt. Everyone would know that Judas was cheap.

Peter was doubtful, prideful, and prone to put his foot in his mouth, yet he survived. Judas was different. He did not take correction well. He was angry that the Lord did not appreciate his opinion. The rebuke proved too much for him. Notice the next verse: *"Then Judas Iscariot, one of the Twelve, went to the chief priests to betray Jesus to them"* (Mark 14:10).

Judas was so offended that he betrayed his Master. I'm sure he rationalized that he was doing Israel a favor. But, deep inside, the real cause of his betrayal was offense. He had been insulted, and now he would get even. And get even he did. Unfortunately, Judas did not know the part he was playing in Satan's plan—a part from which he would never recover.

Can you recognize areas in your life in which you've taken offense? Perhaps a fellow church member hurt you, and you no longer want to go to church. You don't want to see the person who has hurt you. Let's face it: you are trapped. Will you be like Peter and repent, or will you be like Judas and die with bitterness in your heart?

"An offended brother is more unyielding than a fortified city, and disputes are like the barred gates of a citadel" (Proverbs 18:19). It is hard to help an offended brother find emotional and spiritual healing, because of all his resentment. He feels betrayed by others. He is unyielding. It

sometimes seems that there is more hope for the heroin addict than for the offended brother.

You may insist, "You don't understand. He is wrong, and I am right!" Maybe so, but you are trapped, as well. Do you want to be right, or do you want to be free? The choice is yours.

Do you want to be right, or do you want to be free? The choice is yours.

Get free from Satan's power. Don't hold on to your right to be right. Forgive. Let go of all that bitterness. Forgive whoever it was who hurt you or let you down. We are all human. Who are you to judge your brother? Pray the following prayer:

> Father, I see that I am caught in Satan's trap. I need Your help. I have allowed the enemy to magnify the sins of my brothers and sisters. I'm so sorry for letting offense trap me. I forgive anyone whom I think has done me wrong. More important, I ask You to forgive me for my foolishness. I free myself from the trap of the enemy. I have come to my senses. I see the truth. I will walk in forgiveness and peace with my family. In Jesus' name I pray, amen!

Congratulations. You will be the one whom Satan is talking about when he laments, "He was the big fish that got away!"

Part IV

The Evidence

Chapter Twenty

The Power Encounter

I have a deep-seated concern for the body of Christ. If anyone should know the power of Satan and the need to drive him and his cohorts out of people, it is the church. Yet, there is much skepticism within the church about the need for deliverance. The Catholic Church, for example, performs fewer than a dozen exorcisms each year. Surely, there are more than twelve demonized people in their congregations. And what about Protestant churches? They generally shun any encounters with the supernatural. Many Protestants view demons as mere figments of people's imaginations. The age of reason has destroyed the Protestant church's ability to see the need for spiritual deliverance among Christian believers.

There is hope on the horizon. Some evangelicals are finally beginning to explore this vital ministry, but they often fall short of embracing the need for power encounters for Christians. They may believe that demons are real but that they will leave people at salvation. Experience tells me, however, that demons sometimes do not leave completely at the time of salvation. No doubt, salvation is the *beginning* of deliverance, but being born again is not the *end* of deliverance. There is too much biblical evidence to prove that Christians need to remain vigilant against the devil. Demons can influence believers. Of course, unbelievers need deliverance, as well, but until they come to Christ, their deliverance will be short-lived.

> *Salvation is the* **beginning** *of deliverance, but being born again is* **not the** *end of deliverance.*

Recently, more and more evangelicals have begun to realize that Christians can be demonized—not possessed, because the Lord lives in the believer—but demonized, influenced, or controlled to a certain extent by demons.

The best-selling book *The Bondage Breaker* by Neil T. Anderson has brought the evangelical community a long way from the naïve mind-set from which they used to view demons: as being found only in Third World countries where people practice voodoo and worship evil idols. Anderson exposed the church's need for deliverance in the pew—and even the pulpit. Some

Baptists, Methodists, and other Bible-believing Christians embraced the message. Yet, for all the good it did, I believe it fell short in bringing evangelicals to embrace the need for a full-blown deliverance ministry in their churches. Even the author admits,

> I have not attempted to "cast out a demon" in several years. But I have seen hundreds of people find freedom in Christ as I helped them resolve their personal and spiritual conflicts. I no longer deal directly with demons at all, and I prohibit their manifestation.[18]

I am grateful for the "hundreds of people" who have been helped through counseling alone. I believe they truly were helped. But for Mr. Anderson to say that he will "no longer deal directly with demons at all" is not helping the church embrace deliverance. The reason for his methodology is based on his view of a "truth encounter" as opposed to a "power encounter." Anderson writes,

> We have mistakenly regarded freedom as the product of a power encounter instead of a truth encounter. We must avoid buying into Satan's second strategy of power as much as we avoid swallowing his first strategy of deception. It isn't power

---

[18]Neil T. Anderson, *The Bondage Breaker* (Irvine, CA: Harvest House, 2006), 208.

per se that sets the captive free; it's truth. (See John 8:32.)[19]

Anderson sees the need for truth encounters alone. He sees power encounters as passé or perhaps even hurtful. He believes that people only need to hear the Word to be cured of demons.

I am a firm believer in the power of the Word of God. I know that it can set people free from bondage. But I have also seen cases where the power of the Holy Spirit was needed to directly drive out demons. I don't believe—as Anderson does—that truth encounters have made power encounters obsolete. I believe in both. Just as Jesus healed in many ways, I believe there is more than one way to conduct deliverance.

> *If people are able to take hold of the truth of the various solutions God provides for various illnesses, that truth can set them free.*

I think I have demonstrated that if people are able to take hold of the truth of the various solutions God provides for various illnesses, that truth can set them free. Most of this book is based on breaking bondages through the truth of the Word of God. I wrote it in this way because the nature of a book dictates that. I am not present with you. The best I can do to help you is to present the truth—the Word of God. On the other hand, if I were present

---

[19]Anderson, *Bondage Breaker*, 208.

with you, I would probably couple the teaching of the Word with prayers for deliverance. They work together effectively. But since I am not with you, I have to rely on the truth of the message of this book to liberate you. The truth is the Word of God.

In the end, it is not my opinion—or Anderson's—that counts. Look at the Word of God, especially the words of Jesus regarding deliverance: *"But if I drive out demons by the Spirit of God, then the kingdom of God has come upon you"* (Matthew 12:28). Jesus told us how He drove out demons—He did it *"by the Spirit of God."* The Holy Spirit may have inspired the Bible, but Jesus did not drive out demons by using Scripture. He relied on the *power* of the Holy Spirit.

> *Jesus did not drive out demons by using Scripture. He relied on the power of the Holy Spirit.*

In Luke's version of Jesus' statement, it says, *"But if I drive out demons by the finger of God, then the kingdom of God has come to you"* (Luke 11:20). The *"finger of God"* refers to the Holy Spirit. It does not take a huge power surge to drive out demons, simply God's pinkie finger. God's power today remains the same as in Luke's day. Demons flee not solely by His truth, but also by His power.

Look at how the apostles drove out demons:

When Jesus had called the Twelve together, he gave them power and authority to drive out all demons and to cure diseases.

(Luke 9:1)

They received *"power... to drive out all demons."* A "power encounter" was necessary to drive out demons.

I'm not just disappointed in Anderson's lack of reliance on power encounters. What deeply grieves me is that he sees power encounters as "buying into Satan's second strategy of power." I simply choose to drive out demons the way Jesus and the apostles did: through power encounters. Perhaps accepting a lack of power is what truly buys into Satan's strategy.

Why do churches shy away from power encounters? I know it is not due to the Word of God, because the Word advocates power encounters with demons. What, then, could be behind this scheme to keep the church from exercising its dynamic power by driving out demons? I have come up with four primary reasons as to why Christians shy away from power encounters today:

1. The desire to avoid emotional encounters

2. The fear of causing emotional trauma to the candidate for deliverance

3. A skeptical attitude toward miracles

4. Disappointment due to the failure to achieve permanent results

1. *The Desire to Avoid Emotional Encounters*

Power encounters can be messy, emotional experiences. Someone falling on the floor, seething, screaming, crying, and thrashing about is an unusual sight in most churches. Most people don't like to see others in emotional distress, especially in church. Such emotional outbursts make them feel uncomfortable and out of control. They prefer church services to be more predictable and stoic. They like their church gatherings to be composed and well-ordered. Demons, on the other hand, tend to be messy and loud, especially during the deliverance process, which is why many churches opt not to include deliverance in their services.

I believe many churches shy away from power encounters because they cut against the grain of the congregation's personality. I ask you: should people's personalities dictate how God should work in the life of His church? I would encourage those with reserved personalities to get beyond their personal objections in

> *I believe many churches shy away from power encounters because they cut against the grain of the congregation's personality.*

order to recognize the need for a biblical ministry of deliverance. Once they understand its scriptural underpinnings, they may be able to accept it. There are people in my church who are quite reserved yet have learned to accept the workings of God despite their own personalities.

2. The Fear of Causing Emotional Trauma

Some people have real concerns that the ministry of deliverance does more harm than good in the lives of those who need it. These are legitimate concerns, but remember, God's ways are not our ways. (See Isaiah 55:8.) God would never tell us to drive out demons if it would cause others harm.

I have yet to see any evidence that deliverance harms people. On the contrary, psychological studies—as well as my own personal experiences—have proven that people receive positive benefits from prayer for deliverance. People testify that they feel healthy and whole, come closer to God, and are better able to handle everyday problems with new strength.

Of course, I am aware of those who have gone off the deep end in ministering deliverance. I have heard stories of people being held against their wills while biblically illiterate leaders prayed for them. If someone does not want prayer, you should not force it on them. There are also rare cases where people have beaten those who have been demonized. God does not need anyone to use physical force to drive out demons. I have even heard of a case in which a child was forced to drink bleach, as if it had the cleansing power to drive out demons. These are only a few cases of disturbed or ignorant individuals that should not represent the ministries of typical deliverance pastors.

3. A Skeptical Attitude toward Miracles

"Why did you doubt?" (Matthew 14:31). Jesus spoke those words to Peter after he had walked on water but began to sink. Doubt is still the chief reason why people forgo the ministry of deliverance.

Let's face it: most people—even many Christians—doubt the supernatural and are skeptical of demons in general. They know the Bible mentions them, but they rationalize that those verses are simply the superstitious thoughts of unsophisticated people.

> *Doubt is still the chief reason why people forgo the ministry of deliverance.*

Jesus, however, drove out demons. Was He superstitious and unsophisticated? Many Christians, it seems, want to believe in Jesus, but they also want to deny His ministry of deliverance. It embarrasses them. Their doubt has overridden their faith. And the only solution to doubt is faith.

Romans 10:17 says, *"Faith comes from hearing the message, and the message is heard through the word of Christ."* The only way people will ever get rid of their doubt is by hearing the Word of God on the subject. Hopefully, this book will help you overcome your doubt concerning the ministry of deliverance, as well.

4. Disappointment due to the Failure to Achieve Permanent Results

A more likely reason pastors avoid the ministry of deliverance is due to a perceived lack of permanent results in people after they were delivered. I, too, become frustrated when I see people who have received deliverance return to their sins or sicknesses. It's discouraging for any minister when people are unable to maintain their healings.

> *Even though some people may not remain delivered, the truth is, many do maintain their deliverance.*

I would not, however, give up the ministry of deliverance for this reason, any more than I would give up preaching the gospel of salvation simply because people returned to their ungodly ways after coming to Christ. Marriage counselors do not walk away from their practices because some of the couples they counseled end up in divorce.

Jesus told us that demons would try to come back to make matters worse. (See Matthew 12:43–45.) Therefore, it should not come as a surprise when some people do not remain delivered. The truth is, many *do* maintain their deliverance. We need to keep our focus on those who continue to walk in their freedom.

Whatever your reason for shying away from a deliverance ministry, make sure it is a biblical one. If you are honest, you will have to admit that there are no biblical grounds for rejecting the ministry of deliverance. It is biblical, and it works!

Chapter Twenty-one

Real Stories of Deliverance

Many people—including journalists—often ask me if deliverance really works. And they want evidence as proof. Let me share these two stories from people in my church who received healing when they were delivered from evil spirits.

Sandra Carrasco

Sandra Carrasco, a mother of two, is married to Arturo, a successful businessman in the community. Everything seemed normal with this couple, but Sandra was acting anything but normal.

For no apparent reason, thoughts were whirling in her mind. *You have nothing to live for. Just end your life.* One day, she grabbed her keys and took off madly in the car. Her intention was to drive to the nearby mountains, where she would kill herself by driving off one of the cliffs.

Determined to end her life, she wove in and out of traffic until she noticed another car following closely behind her. It was mimicking her every move. She attempted to lose it, but it stayed on her tail. Although the car was behind her, it seemed to Sandra as if it was controlling her driving. Finally, she turned off the road into a church parking lot. When she turned around, the other car had vanished.

Sandra was exhausted. She thought, *What am I going to do?* Then, another thought occurred to her. *I need to call my pastor.*

As soon as I picked up the phone, I could tell that Sandra was distraught. She did not sound like herself. I told her to come to my house.

When she arrived, she was still in a daze. My wife, Sonia, and I invited her in and immediately began to ask questions. She confessed that she wanted to end her life. Sonia and I tried to encourage her, but we quickly realized that we needed to drive the demons from her.

As Sandra sat on our couch, Sonia stood next to her, and I proceeded to lay my hands on her head. I began to command every demon to leave her life. As I did, Sandra screamed. The demons were yelling, "No!" Sandra slid down the couch until she was lying on her back. I continued to hover over her, still commanding the demons to leave. A battle was waging within her soul. Her hands were flailing back and forth, but not once did Sonia or I get hit. God protected us from any physical harm.

After about ten minutes, the demons were gone. Sandra came out of her daze and smiled. She knew she had been delivered. This all occurred more than sixteen years ago, and today, Sandra is a member of our church.

My Mother

For decades, my mother, Billie, kept her devastating battle with the disease of bulimia from our family. She was too embarrassed to admit that for over twenty years, she had regularly vomited her food. To her, it was a way of remaining in control of her weight, but, in reality, it was the disease that was controlling her.

Health professionals tell us that there is no cure for bulimia. The best they hope for is that psychological counseling will somehow decrease the desire to vomit. God, however, is able to remove bulimia completely.

I remember feeling especially anointed on the Sunday when my mother came forward for prayer. Boldness was on me in an extraordinary way. I called for people to come forward if they needed the Lord to deliver them from evil spirits.

To my surprise, one of the three who came forward was my own mother.

As she came toward the front, I thought, *What could she possibly need deliverance from?* In her eyes, however, I could see the desperation, which quickly turned to tears. As I prayed for those three who had come forward, my mother began to shake uncontrollably. She let out a few gasps. Later, she said that she felt an awful presence leave her body. *Could that have been a demon?* she thought. It was! After twenty years, she was finally free.

Now, more than eighteen years after her deliverance, my mother has not vomited since, including any bouts of influenza. Healing came to her through deliverance.

About the Author

Tom Brown is best known for his deliverance ministry. He has been featured on ABC's *20/20*, as well as on programs on MSNBC and the History Channel, which featured his ministry of deliverance and highlighted his success in dealing with the spiritually oppressed. Although people view him as an "exorcist," he personally shuns the title and prefers to be known as a down-to-earth pastor. He founded Word of Life Church in El Paso, Texas, with only seven members. Now, its congregation numbers over 1,500 members.

Tom has authored several books and is known in El Paso through his many local television appearances. The rest of the world knows him through his award-winning home page, www.tbm.org, which receives over a million visitors a year.